AWAKENING
~BY~
GRIEF

LIZ HERNANDEZ

Awakening by Grief
Copyright © 2020 by Liz Hernandez

All rights reserved. No part of this publication may be reproduced, distributed, or transmitted in any form or by any means, including photocopying, recording, or other electronic or mechanical methods, without the prior written permission of the author, except in the case of brief quotations embodied in critical reviews and certain other non-commercial uses permitted by copyright law.

Tellwell Talent
www.tellwell.ca

ISBN
978-0-2288-2800-6 *(Hardcover)*
978-0-2288-2799-3 *(Paperback)*
978-0-2288-2801-3 *(eBook)*

DEDICATION

This book is dedicated to:

The Divine and the Spiritual realm.

My children—Giovanni for believing in me and

Oriliz because she always supported me.

My family—brothers, sisters, nephews, and nieces.

My dad, Augusto, for all his fantastic stories which

have always inspired my imagination.

Love and Light! ♡

TABLE OF CONTENTS

Acknowledgments ix
Introduction xi
Chapter 1   The Beginning 1
Chapter 2   Agony 9
Chapter 3   The Grieving 15
Chapter 4   Denial 19
Chapter 5   Her Absence 21
Chapter 6   The Illness 25
Chapter 7   My Grief as a Mom 31
Chapter 8   Death 39
Chapter 9   My Son, Giovanni 47
Chapter 10   Her Endeavours and Her Charisma 51
Chapter 11   Rest in Peace 59
Chapter 12   My Spiritual Path—The Awakening 61

Poems 77
Afterword 83
About The Author 87

But they who wait for the Lord shall renew their strength; they shall mount up with wings like eagles; they shall run and not be weary; they shall walk and not faint.

—**Isaiah 40:31**

ACKNOWLEDGMENTS

Thank you to:

Giovanni for encouraging me and continuing to light up my life with laughter.

All my daughter's friends for caring and always being in touch.

Keith, to continue with the friendship.

Gloria and Lorraine, for giving me their free time to talk about the book.

My friends, co-workers, and acquaintances who have been supporters in my grief and to everyone else who has given me courage with their presence and kind words, especially Nadia, Isabelle R, and Lorraine.

Johnny for being my best friend.

I will always be forever grateful; I would not have managed without your help and support. Again, thank you so much.

ORILIZ,

Our fear is we will forget you because we won't see you again or feel your perfume in the air or hear your beautiful voice when you are arriving home. We must accept your departure because it is God's will, but at the same time, we thank him for all the happy and sad moments we have shared with you.

We are proud to be your family. We miss you!

We love you, daughter, sister, granddaughter, niece, cousin, friend, forever!

INTRODUCTION

I felt the need to write this book because the pain was unbearable. Even though I would get a knot in my throat just thinking about it, I thought if I wrote this book, the pain would go away and maybe I could have peace or closure. I did it for my own good: for my own mental, physical and emotional state.

The loss of my daughter made me shift my life to a huge dimension that I never knew. The loneliness, the suffering and the emptiness in my heart because of the lack of her love made me hide in my own shadow for a long period of time; I hid in the silence and the quiet suffering of my soul.

I felt lonely and deceived by God and the whole world. I did not want to live anymore because of the sharp pain in my chest. I wanted to be with her. This is a feeling that even if I want to explain, it is impossible; and it had nothing to do with depression. I felt empty especially when I closed my eyes to see her face again. I used to see dark, and I used to see nothing. I could not see the beautiful moments or any other nice experiences we had had together since darkness had enveloped my heart with a big black cloud of regret and guilt.

I prayed, I prayed and I prayed to see her again: to see her beautiful face, to touch her soft skin, to hear her voice of love again, to see her sweet smile; and I prayed every day after going to bed, and then I would sleep deeply...

I became quiet and an observer of life during this healing process. I let everything go with the flow and fall into place.

Finally, my prayers were answered: I had my dream. I saw her in the thin air with her hair still curly but longer, dressed in a long bluish-purple robe. She was talking to me, telling me, *"Thank you for everything.*

You are strong and I understand now. I thought I was supporting you, but it was you who supported me. That's why I chose you to lead my death. Take care of Giovanni and help my dad to heal for me to continue my path. Love you all."

At that moment, I thought it was a dream, but my body felt it. It was a feeling I could never describe; I felt happy and sad at the same time, but I saw her; God had granted my wish!

Everything in me started to change. I started to come out of the shadows slowly. My mind was starting to get clear and lucid. I started to live again, but with the pain still in me! Now I needed to work on the pain, but how?

Five years following her death, I decided to tell my story to other moms and dads who have lost their children. I feel their pain, their sorrow and their sadness, and I know that I am not alone. I felt deep in my heart that they were like me—not accepting of this situation and looking for an escape.

It is my intention this book will help parents like me find some closure to their sorrow, as I have. Probably if they understand what I went through, it will give them a little bit of peace to continue with their life; at least for those that are still here. I feel for those people that lost their lives because they could not find calmness, peace and tranquillity during the grief of their own child.

We, as parents, are put on Earth to guide, to comfort, to teach, and to love our children. We must make sure they are doing well in this life. We want to see them following the best path possible and to see them get married and have children as we once did. But, as a parent, there is no book of instructions that you can follow; it is just the feelings of caring, patience, and love that we radiate to our children that will make the difference.

We, as parents, can do our best, but believe me, we cannot do our best when we lose them. Our hope, our effort, and our future become so narrow, so limited and so dark. The experience of losing a child clouds our mind, our thoughts and any possibility of existence.

There are no words to describe this feeling; there are no medications to heal the pain; there are no happy moments that would heal your thoughts. The child could be a baby, a youngster, or an adult young or old; regardless, it is hard to accept. Some people do it, and others do not. The sadness invades your soul for a long time...

I can only tell you that my children are my world, my life. We, as parents, change our whole experience to create a new one for our children; we want to create something new for them so they can adapt in life. We want to show them—*This is us, our perfect world; love it because we are here too. We will never let you down, we will never hide from you, and we will fight life together. Because we are together! That's our job to fight as a family.*

Imagine that enthusiasm for our children, for our new group that we have created. It is worth it! We will have setbacks, we will have some fights, arguments and at the same time some laughs, but we are still a family. We will go to infinity and back just for answers and solutions for our children. That is our role, as parents.

When you lose a member of that group, especially a child, that group crumbles. All those beautiful days, ugly days and even the big arguments come to mind in a second. Those memories make you feel regret and sadness.

We thought one rule existed: the older ones die first, the younger ones die later, but the universe disagrees.

Losing them is the hardest and last thing we expect from life. Believe me! We, as parents, are prepared for anything, but the death of our most precious gift of life—our children—make us go into darkness...

CHAPTER 1

The Beginning

I came to Montreal on September 3, 1980, for the first time. I was eighteen when my dad approved of my decision. He was hesitant to let me come to an unknown city. They always thought this was the North Pole where Santa Claus lived, metaphorically.

I came with the son of one of my mom's best friend's. He was studying at Concordia University. Concordia University has an international program in the Continuing Education faculty focused on teaching languages to young people from around the world. We were from everywhere: Mexico, Venezuela, Salvador, Chile, Argentina, Greece, Italy, Iran, Iraq, Romania, etc. We all gathered at the same time at the registration centre for the English program starting that September. I had made it just in time. I met so many new people from around the world, and I made a few friends during my time at Concordia University.

I lived on Sherbrooke Street close to Loyola campus where my mom's best friend's son was studying. I used to take the bus which brought me to the Atwater subway station. It was an adventure for me since everything was new and beautiful. Sometimes, I would take the metro up and down the route just to know the stations. I knew the metro by heart and even the buses. This was my first time as an independent young person. I loved it!

I did not know what to expect on this trip. I was afraid but at the same time excited and enthusiastic. I had the thrill of knowing this beautiful country that I had heard about my entire life from my old friends at Central University in Venezuela.

On the first day of class, I met a young blond boy, Danny, his sister Rose **(+)** and two of their friends who were already a couple. Rose was a nice and beautiful girl. After she went back to Venezuela and made her dream come true, she died unexpectedly. For me, it was very sad. I cried, and then I thought about her brother Danny who loved her so much!

We always gathered outside of the university or in the apartment of anyone who decided to receive noisy young people. We used to speak about everything, starting with: What to do tonight? It was weird because, finally, I started doing what my brothers and sisters used to do: Party time! I was not too much into that, but it helped to fade away the nostalgic pain I had from missing my family and my country. I spent time in Discos dancing and drinking with moderation, especially on the weekends. During the week, we were just learning English or French as full-time students and we were having fun in our free time.

In school, I met a student, through my friend Sal from Mexico, in the English advanced course. He had come from the USA, but he was an Italian Venezuelan. His name was Stefano. I found him cute and sexy. I started talking to him and discovered he was a party animal like me. I got along with him, together with my friend Sal; we decided to discover the Montreal nightlife!

Almost every student had their apartments on the streets of downtown. I was the only one who lived in Sherbrooke West. Sometimes I spent time in my friend's apartments after school. I was so naive and inexperienced that anybody could have taken advantage of me at any time. I think my face and my expression showed it, but nobody mentioned anything. Wherever I went I found Venezuelan students and everyone knew my dad. I was miles away from my country, and here in Montreal, I found people who knew my dad. *I knew my dad was famous, but not that famous! I guess I was wrong!* I used to say silently.

My English course was only eight months long, and I had already completed four months; my interest in Stefano was growing stronger.

We used to go out, drink and sleep together and all the beautiful thoughts invaded my head. I think I loved him. Love at first sight!

One day, I did not feel right. I felt pain in my right leg, and I didn't know what to do if I needed to see a doctor. I asked Danny, who was the expert because he lived here longer than any of us. He explained that I had to go to a smaller clinic because they would always have a doctor onsite. Those clinics were very efficient. They were the community clinics that were all around Montreal, depending on where you lived. I decided to go because it was weird that the pain did not go away. When the doctor was checking, he started talking about sex, relationships, protection, pregnancy, etc. I was embarrassed. It was not a conversation I could have because I did not have a vocabulary for it. Talking about sex and the whole thing that goes with that was taboo in my house. I didn't know how to answer the doctor...

The news of my pregnancy came as a bucket of cold water. I didn't know what to do. I didn't know who to tell. I was very disappointed in myself. I wanted to stay in Canada, graduate and get married. It was too much to ask after this news. I told Stefano, and he didn't know what to do either. We were children. We had dreams and goals. Everything came crashing down... I guess.

We decided to keep it quiet while we completed the remaining four-month English course. My friend Sal was the only one who knew what was happening. He even wanted to be the godfather. Sal was always a happy man. Always making jokes and flirted with all the girls at the university. He met a girl from Greece and then it became serious.

For a while, we were going to Stefano's parent's house. We would spend weekends there. For us, coming from the downtown area to the East area of Montreal was like going to a house in the country. Even though we used to take the metro and bus, it was far. I think Stefano did not know how to tell his parents about the pregnancy. We lied for a while. We were saying that Sal was my boyfriend and I was pregnant. It did not last long. Sal needed to go back to Mexico because his dad got sick. The truth came out...

Living with his parents was not what I wanted, but I was grateful that at least I had a place to stay and I would have my baby to keep me company. His father spoke to my dad. My dad was not upset with me. He understood and let us get married. This was one of the most disappointing moments of my life—to let my dad down who I love so much! I respected the man who taught me everything. He worked hard to pay for my schooling in Montreal, and this was the way I was paying him back. One day I will explain to him why this happened!

I was nineteen and married to Stefano when my water broke. I was rushed to the hospital. I got there with no pain. The nurse who had been helping me with the maternal care classes was by my side. She was repeating the contraction exercises with me. The pain became intense after thirty hours of labour. The doctor finally came and said, "Prepare her for a cesarean." The pain in my back did not stop. It felt like somebody was breaking my back with their bare hands. I was yelling my lungs out until, finally, the general anesthesia invaded my whole body. I did not see or hear anything anymore. I woke up, and I was out of the operating room with pain in my back, my neck, and my legs. A nurse came to see me and told me that I had a beautiful daughter. I heard her say, "It looks like children having children." But I would not have changed that experience for anything. I finally slept for a few hours until they brought my daughter to my room. The nurse was trying to teach me how to breastfeed my daughter, but with no success. After many attempts, we decided to give her the bottle with my breast milk. It was better that way since my breasts were not large.

The day my daughter was born, December 21, 1981, there was a storm in Montreal. Thirty-five centimetres of snow fell, and the hill to the Montreal General Hospital was very slippery by car. My husband was unable to get there to visit me. Three days passed and the storm persisted. I felt abandoned by Stefano, and I started doubting the relationship.

Finally, my husband came when I was released. He visited me and his daughter. He spent quite a long time with us until it was time to leave. Everything was checked before leaving: my scar, the baby and the instructions.

We took many pictures of my baby daughter. We even celebrated because she was the first baby from the first Italian male. It was good but at the same time, the family was disappointed because she was not a boy. In the Italian custom, if the first male has a boy as his firstborn, there is a big celebration. It is like a big thing for them. Well, this time she was for me, my big celebration.

For me, boy or girl, it was my first child. I never felt as happy as that day. I remembered the pain that I went through, but everything was worth it. I had a baby. But now, my next step was to find a name.

I wanted to create a name. I wanted something beautiful since my daughter was beautiful. I wanted something for everyone to remember. I combined names. I tried many combinations from my mother's name, Lourdes, and from my husband's mother, Oria. Nothing worked out. Then I combined my mother-in-law's name with mine to create Ori + Liz = **ORILIZ.** That was a gorgeous name—a beautiful name that would last forever and nobody would forget it.

Oriliz's Apgar score (results of test administered minutes after birth to assess newborn's health) was seven. Oriliz could not cry properly after being in distress during pregnancy. The doctor recommended letting her cry for a few minutes before attending to her as a way to help her develop her lungs. Oriliz was always sleeping because she was low in iron and she did not have an appetite. Other than that, she was healthy. Oriliz was a happy child and very joyful when she was growing up. We never had any problems with attitude or foolishness. She was a good child, and she was attentive to everything that happened around her. Oriliz was bright and playful. I think she came to this earth for a reason. One of them was to make us happy, especially her dad. She and her dad were always together. She even cried for him when he would leave for work. Oriliz loved her dad so much. Sometimes, she woke up when her dad arrived from work. She used to spend time with him, eating together, making funny gestures, and they were always laughing and waking up the whole family. These were nice days. Beautiful ones!!

My divorce happened when Oriliz was nine. She wanted to go live with her father because of her brother. My son was six when the court decided to change his home. My daughter also wanted to go live with her brother. I agreed. I let them go if it was for their happiness. The decision left me with the most sadness that I have ever felt.

The divorce was tough and hard to bear. I did wonders, being in many places at once. I depended on Montreal's transportation but at the time it was slow and without a schedule. Sometimes I had setbacks because of unfortunate events. These events were produced by hateful and sometimes unhappy people. I would get home feeling hopeless, without strength, with a pain in my chest, crying with anger and asking God for help. I just wanted to be in a peaceful mood to see my children. No interference. No comments. No discouragement. No insults.

I took a trip to Venezuela for a few months. I wanted to disconnect from the whole situation. I was not defeated yet. I just wanted to prepare my next move. I didn't know where to start. The trip did me well. I connected with my family again, and I saw that my mom was very sick at the time. I used to argue with my mom all the time. Sometimes I thought she hated me, but I never knew for certain because she died a few years later. I could not handle the discord anymore with my mom; I decided to come back to Montreal to see my children again.

After the trip to Venezuela, my luck started to change. I went to college and graduated from Dawson College in language and literature. I wanted to pursue a carrier in law, languages or teaching. Those were my choices. I would see what the future held for me!

Life is full of surprises because after much hustle, a lot of crying, and many discomforts with the world around me I could not go to university. I was diagnosed with systemic lupus erythematosus disease, a long-term autoimmune disease in which the body's immune system becomes hyperactive and attacks normal, healthy tissue, commonly known as lupus.

I was thirty-two when I was diagnosed with Lupus. I got pericarditis, which is an infection in the pericardium, the membrane which lubricates the heart for its movements. I lost my languages. I started to speak slowly again. I had to learn English and French words again. Oriliz would remind me of a word whenever I was stuck. Now I even have an accent; I did not have one before. I could not speak properly. I had to take a French course to remember my vocabulary again. I found my rhythm with the languages, slowly but surely.

I started to learn about Lupus. I studied the illness and I joined the lupus association. I asked my family about the disease and since my mom had died of lupus, I got my answers. I also found some information about the disease, and I found out that with precaution and discipline you can live longer.

My life changed after all the unforeseen misfortune. I started to live a responsible life. I was looking for serious jobs. I worked three jobs at the same time. I was saving money and started looking at long-term commitments in my life. I was thinking more about my children, and I decided to take the whole situation more seriously. I started to negotiate with life, and I was getting all this help from my surroundings. I was getting what I wanted, but sometimes I was disappointed, though it was fair too!

I continued my everyday life as normally as possible. I used to find people who helped me on my way up, and I used to find disappointment too. It was not easy to reach the level that I am at now. I pursued all this because I needed to show my children that I was a good person. I was very responsible, and I wanted them in my life. Whatever the world was saying about me, I wanted to prove them wrong. I wanted to prove to my children that the world was very torn, indecisive and enraged. I wanted to let them know that they could count on this human, me. This human was not going anywhere. They could have me forever and ever. Then, I promised myself to be here for them until death do us part!

At the time, I believed that life was full of setbacks and this was the way to continue in life. However, as I got older something used to tell me that that was not true. Life was easier than this. There is something bigger than us creating reality. This was an experience to learn and nothing else. But what I did not know was that the toughest experience would be on its way years later. Life was preparing me for something bigger than those small setbacks. Life was preparing me for something more painful and awful.

CHAPTER 2

Agony

It was 9:00 a.m., February 4, 2014, when they came to pick Oriliz up. I feared the future. I did not know if it was the last time I would see her. My body was shaking; it was announcing something that I was unsure of. On the way to the elevator, she and I were crying for no reason—I think because of the unknown. I tried to control the situation by telling her that everything would be all right, even though my heart was throbbing full of doubts. My head was thinking all the negative thoughts: *What if it was not all right?* We knew the risk, but it was not the time to lose her now. From that moment on, the anguish invaded my soul. I prayed to God once, twice and many times. I was fearful of losing Oriliz, but at the same time, I was confident that she would get out of this one. I was confused...

After many hours of waiting, from the morning to the evening, finally, I got the news that everything was a success; I thanked God. Something inside me told me not to believe it until I see her again. The doctor was very confident that the operation was a success and that she would get out of this. "Anyway, your daughter is young and healthy, so why not?" the doctor said.

I waited and waited, past midnight, until I finally saw Oriliz. She looked tired and downhearted. I thought it must be because of the long day of unpleasant emotions. I spoke Spanish and I said, "Baby, everything is all right."

"I am thirsty," she replied in French. I was skeptical that all the danger had passed. My body was still shaking inside, giving me signs of something, but I ignored it. The nurse told me that I could give her small pieces of ice instead of water, which I did. Oriliz asked for her friend, and I answered her that he was not there but that her father and brother were outside. Oriliz was awake, even though the medication was kicking in. She asked if I would take a picture of her. She mentioned that she would open her eyes for the picture. I laughed, but I did take it. We let her rest...

I went to get a coffee, and I finally relaxed. I fell into the chair as if somebody had strongly pushed me. I felt good, but at the same time I was tired. I started looking at the photo I had taken, and I saw Oriliz lying down in her hospital bed with her hair on top of the pillow and her eyes wide open. I started to ask myself: *Why does Oriliz want this photo taken? Does she want people to see this photo later, maybe to remember her? Why?* I told myself: *Oh, Liz, you are exaggerating.* I went to check on Oriliz for the last time, and I left for home. A sadness enveloped my body without knowing why.

On February 5, early in the morning, I went to see Oriliz again. I entered the intensive care unit as many times as I pleased, but as she was still drugged, she moved slowly and tried sometimes to open her eyes. In the afternoon, the doctors decided to change Oriliz to a room on the fourth floor since she was responding well to the medication. I asked, "Why? Is it not too soon? Isn't it a mistake?" The doctor in charge answered that they needed space for others that were coming out of the operating room.

They were preparing Oriliz to bring her upstairs when I was at lunch at the cafeteria of the St-Luc hospital. I finished my sandwich and my coffee, and I went upstairs to intensive care and the nurse told me: "She has been moved to a room on the fourth floor. She is in a two-patient room where she will be comfortable." I could not believe it, but at this moment, there was nothing I could do. I was alone, and the doctors were deciding her destiny for now.

I went up and I saw Oriliz. She was sleeping... I rested in an empty chair and I dreamt with my eyes open until my ex-husband showed up...

On February 6, Oriliz was still drugged with medication. She woke up a little bit, just to tell me to call the nurse because she as a nurse herself knew something was wrong. Oriliz mentioned to the nurse that she wanted to see the doctor. She wanted to stop the medication that made her drowsy. The nurse did not want to bother the doctor, but my daughter explained to the nurse that she wanted to feel better to speak to her family. When the nurse shook her head of disapproval, Oriliz got upset and the nurse called the doctor without hesitation. The doctor gave the nurse the order to remove the medication.

Oriliz started to come to her senses a little bit. She told me that she had a headache and to put a small wet washcloth in her head. She started asking questions. She asked for her dad, her brother and her friend "K." I told her that they were coming the next day, but she nodded her head like she knew that she would not see them again. My fears came back like a heat in my body and then cold...

Oriliz pointed out that she could not breathe. She wanted to sit down, and she wanted me to help her. She told me what to do for her exercises. All this happened without the nurse there. Oriliz was strong and a very knowledgeable nurse. She knew her career from A to Z. She knew what she felt, and she wanted to prove it wrong with the exercises, but I guess she could not.

I told her, "It is better if I call the nurse."

She answered, "I will tell you what to do."

I helped her and did what she told me to do. She sat in the bed, supported by my arms. She breathed in and out twice, and I could see her eyes go big when she inhaled. Then she lay down. I asked her, "So, what happened?"

Oriliz, being a nurse, knew what was happening. With her index finger, she pointed, using left and right movements, that she would not make it to the next day.

I said, "Please, do not believe that."

In a hoarse voice, she said, "Go home, Mom."

I saw her chin wrinkle. I saw her sadness! She knew...

I kissed Oriliz, without knowing that was the last time that I would see her alive. I told her, "I love you," and I went to call the nurse.

The hospital was not a nice hospital when it came to interactions with the family. The room was a mess and the other patient was mentally ill and had no consideration for her roommate. She was talking loudly, especially when she got phone calls. The son who accompanied the lady asked her many times to lower her voice but without success. I asked the nurse if it was possible to change my daughter to another room since she was not feeling well, and she needed to rest. The nurse answered, "This is not the Queen Elizabeth Hotel. We cannot move people to another room." I was full of mixed feelings. I sighed...

Around 11:30 p.m., I saw that Oriliz was sleeping. I touched her body, her hands. I kissed her again, and I rubbed her head and I said, "I will go home, and I will come back right away."

Around midnight, the nurse came to check Oriliz's vital signs. She saw the oxygen was going down and she brought it up a little bit. At that moment, the nurse called the doctor and my daughter was transferred immediately to the intensive care unit again. All these decisions were done without my knowledge. I was home praying for her recovery. I lay down in my bed, and I crashed...

The hospital mentioned that they were trying to call me but that the number was wrong. My son and my ex-husband showed up at the hospital to visit my daughter when, finally, they called me to come to the hospital since Oriliz was not doing well. I was at an early appointment, but my body told me to leave and to run to the hospital. I did not know how to drive. My body was shaking, and I wanted to go before she died. I wanted to see her eyes for one last time. I wanted to tell her that I was there, and she was not alone.

When I arrived at the hospital, I was running down the hall to take the elevator, and on the way out of the elevator, I found the doctor crushed. I already knew what my body was telling me: *She will not make it*. The doctor said, "The team is working on her; I hope she makes it."

On February 7, 2014, my daughter passed on, after being revived many times. She knew she was ready to leave us, back in the room. Those were the last words and gestures that I exchanged with my daughter. Oriliz never saw her brother, or K, or her father a last time. I imagined her soul above us or walking among us, telling us that she was okay or that she was terrified and did not want to leave. Who would know?

Sometimes, I imagined if Oriliz had felt so bad physically that she let go or that she embraced her courage to die because it would be very difficult to leave this world at her age and being conscious of the surroundings.

In a way, Oriliz knew that she would leave us. She knew that our life here was without her. Oriliz left all her personal things in order, she had a reunion with her best friends, and she said goodbye to everyone by text.

Oriliz passed on February 7, 2014, at the age of thirty-two.. She made our life radiant and happy for thirty-two years. We will miss her forever!

CHAPTER 3

The Grieving

It took us a while to digest the news. The doctor came to see us in the small room where they talked to families. I feared the words, but I knew that last night was the last kiss. I could not see or think straight. When the doctor said the news, my tears came out and my state of denial kicked in. We told the doctor that we wanted to see her, and he said, "In a few minutes. They are taking out the probes."

When I saw Oriliz's body in the small, cold room, I said in Spanish, "Aw, my daughter, how they left you," and my tears started forming. I began to cry heavily. My feelings were a mixture of anger and sadness and everything together. I touched her body and it was hot and soft. Her eyes were out a little, as she was angry from the force of the defibrillator; her chest was bowled as if she had fought for the last breath. The blood was coming out of her nose as she had exploded inside, and her skin had little brown spots if her purpura had come back. This is not a nice image to keep of your child, especially as the last image. I kept this image for a while and sometimes that is what I remember. I tried to forget it, but it was impossible. When I came to my senses, I started to see around the room. My son was sitting to her right, crying. My ex and his new wife were sitting to her left, crying. And then, silence...

The silence was broken by cell phones ringing and murmurs of friends waiting outside. Outside most of her closest friends were waiting to see her. We tried to fix her up, drying the blood to show no trail, but with no success. Her closest friends wanted to see Oriliz for the last time. They came in, but anyone who saw her in that shape was impacted. I thought if I cleaned her nose, they would have had a different scene, but it was not my choice.

People were asking me about the whole situation by text messages and phone calls; I didn't know what to do, who to blame or where to go. Phones were ringing for the news. Some people were horrified by the news of her death, while others had predicted it. I never expected something like this to be happening to me. I saw myself immune to these kinds of things. I never knew what it felt like to be in a situation like this. I did not want to see people around me, telling me, "Courage." It was complicated for me—more than I thought...

I remember telling my sister and one of my daughter's friends about her death; the screaming that they let out reached my whole body, from my ears to my toes. I felt the agony of those people; I guess it was painful for them. I could see how important my daughter was to them. I felt stupid for a few minutes, but my denial did not go away. It stayed, bothering me all along...

I went to speak to the doctor, and he explained to me how everything had happened. I heard him talking and I saw that he did not read Oriliz's files. He did not know anything about the patient that was my daughter. He did not know that my daughter had a do not resuscitate declaration. She also had purpura, a deadly disease that she needed a transfusion for to help her live. Neither of those factors had been taken into consideration. They did not know anything. They operated on her, and then sent her to a room where the unit was not equipped for what she had been operated for; they were short on beds in the intensive care unit and they needed her out even though she was not ready. They killed her! Who knows the truth, only themselves? My daughter was a nurse, and she knew that the system was not perfect. That is why she wanted off the medication, so she could control her surroundings. She did not trust the system. All of this was overwhelming for me.... I needed to rest!

I went back to the small cold room where her body was getting cold. My ears were ringing as somebody was talking to me desperately. I said to my daughter mentally, *I don't understand. Please find my mom; she will guide you,*" and then I looked up to the room's ceiling. I felt a peace...

We did not want to leave, something was pulling me to stay, but they came to tell us to go to the registration office. The office felt sad and grey. The employee was asking questions related to her autopsy. He made us sign some papers for legal procedures and that was the end of the hospital days. We went in with some hope and we left with none. The hospital gave us more doubts and sadness than ever. I wondered if my daughter felt the same. My soul was screaming in pain when I was leaving the hospital. At the same time I was cursing its staff and doctors and their attitude toward the patients. I felt defeated.

CHAPTER 4

Denial

Now I started to speak to my daughter from inside out, in that empty cold room: *Oriliz, I see that everything has calmed down now. I got surprised that you are not talking to me. Just yesterday I said goodbye and I kissed you. Everything is a nightmare, you know! At this moment I would like to go back to yesterday and see you again, one last time.*

I continued, *Only the ones who shared your life with you are around you. They miss you already! I can't continue with the strange pain, slowly covering my whole body. I can't continue having this deep pain in my heart, telling me that you are not here anymore!* Thoughts invaded my mind, I wanted to scream: *Wake up! You are not dead! You are kidding me! Tell me how to continue my life without you. How to laugh without you. Oriliz, how to find happiness again in this world since it doesn't make sense to me anymore. Look up, you, so sad in that bed. I don't want to see you that way!!! I love you. Wake up!!*

In my thoughts at that moment I said, *I want to tell you how hot the blood feels running in my veins. I want to scream. What should I do? How should I let you go? Should I run? Somebody help me. Why this is happening to me? How many more years until I see you again? How do I go thirty-two more years without you? How? Help, please? Help me? Aw!*

I did not stop: *I miss you already, your smell, your voice, your laugh and also your kisses. They are still alive in my mind. I still don't believe it. How could a person, a strong nurse with dreams, lose everything in one day, a day like today, February 7, 2014. How come? Explain please, please...*

The images of your dead body are registered in my mind: the moment your body changed from hot to cold, the expression in your face of letting me go and your soft small hands when I touched them. It seems that you are asleep, nothing more.

Those memories are still as fresh in my brain as if it was yesterday. I was shocked and in denial. That moment for me is a perpetual pain hidden in the core of my body and it does not go away. It feels intense, but as soon as it finds its way out, it will exit in propulsion. However, this is what makes me more vulnerable to life. There is no way to heal these wounds. I just camouflage them for a better life but not for a cheerful one...

I called her many times on her cell phone, just to hear her voice message. I had some text messages from the weeks before her operation which I read many, many times. In those texts, I saw that at that moment, she was happy and making jokes about everything that she found funny. I watched some videos from when she had gone to Scotland, just to hear her voice again, talking and laughing. I went over and over them until my brain could not handle it anymore. I became defensive of her. I became her protector. I became the denial of her non-existence.

CHAPTER 5

Her Absence

If we ask the doctors and the hospital all our questions, they do not have the answers. When it comes to death nobody knows what happens or what they could do better to save someone's life. We know when we are born because it is the most beautiful moment. The reaction of parents when they see their beautiful baby for the first time is priceless. However, nobody knows when death will happen: just the day that it happens, and there is nothing one can do. There are always complications when you are dying because that is your day until death decides it is your last hour. The memories from death are left with us. It is only a body without a soul that will fade from your mind with time.

Nobody, family or friend, is prepared for a death in this lifetime. Some of us will get stronger and continue with our lives as if nothing happened, but some of us, like me, will miss those memories and never go back to our lives before. It is hard to continue. Normal life will cease to exist. All the previous days, the moments of beautiful memories, are your priorities in bad weather, in dreams, on special occasions and even, in specific moments.

It is so hard for us to continue without our children. The feeling is like missing one part of our body but inside out. The pain is unbearable; I cannot explain the feeling. I know that your mind, body, and soul are connected at the same time with pain. The whole body aches, worse than arthritis. You tried to find answers from somewhere, anywhere, just to feel better because you know that deep in your heart, life continues!

For me, Oriliz was the light of my house. She was my daughter, my friend, my confidante and more. I felt an attachment to her from being here for a long time with me. I thank God for giving me the chance to have her for four more years after her crisis in 2010. I always took care of her like she was a baby. She was a very good friend to her friends. She remembered everyone's birthday; she was there for them anytime. That was Oriliz. Anyone you ask about Oriliz will tell you what a funny and social person she was, always sharing and being part of the group. She had no fear whatsoever of talking or saying what she meant. Her outgoing personality is what you would see as soon as she entered a room.

Her loss is painful for the family, especially the ones close to her. We miss Oriliz every day of our lives, especially now that the years have passed. We remember her as if she moved to another country and that she will soon get in touch with us. We do not even notice that she has died unless a glimpse of a memory appears, and then, we realize it. It has only been five years since she left us. At every commemorated event, such as birthdays, weddings, Christmas, New Year's, or any other celebration, we all have Oriliz on our minds. We all say, "She is here with us."

In 2013 we celebrated with a lot of joy because we didn't know what 2014 would bring us. We shared happy moments of her life. The next year, 2014, was not a happy year; we didn't share anything because that year was full of agony, sadness, and deceptions. When 2014 opened its door, we didn't know it was opening it for Oriliz to travel without a return ticket. I still think that she knew the outcome. Everyone was there celebrating with her to say goodbye for her long journey without coming back. We never knew if she was leaving for the last time. Who would think that 2014 would be the last year for her? At only thirty-two years old? The pain of all of this is that we are not going to see her for the first 365 days and years to come. But when a year comes, a challenge opens for us. Not only now, forever!!!!

If her soul looked down at that precise moment, when she died, when we were all together in that cold room, I am sure she gave us her last goodbye. She knows now what our souls felt from her departure: an infinite love. She saw our tears drop with a lot of pain, and a long thought of grieving for her long departure. She left us melancholy, lonely, glooming and anxious.

Every parent wants wellness for their children, so I hope Oriliz is happy and laughing, and what I am sure of is that she is no longer suffering.

Scotland 2013

CHAPTER 6

The Illness

In 2010, Oriliz realized her body was full of blues. As a nurse herself, she had an idea of what she had, but like always she thought it would go away. She had no idea her life was in danger.

She decided to see the doctor where she used to work, and he told her to go to the hospital immediately. Her platelet count was low. I never found out how low it was, but I knew it was at a dangerous level. When she reached the hospital, she fainted on the floor in the emergency room. The ER personnel brought her inside where they induced coma and intubated her right away. Dr. Ima, trying to save her life, asked us questions about her recent trip to Mexico. She had travelled there a month earlier. I thought to myself the same thing. I thought: *Oh, she got dengue* (a potentially fatal disease transmitted by mosquitos to humans).

After many medical tests the doctor told me that she did not have dengue, she had idiopathic thrombocytopenic purpura (ITP), a rare blood disorder that can lead to easy or excessive bruising and bleeding due to an unusually low platelet count. (Platelets are tiny blood cells that help the blood form clots.) In Oriliz's case, the clots were so small, Dr. Ima was afraid they would spread throughout her body. ITP is very dangerous for the brain, heart, and even lungs. Any clot in her body could kill her if the doctor was not careful to find them. This first time, Dr. Ima, a hematologist, saved her life. Dr. Ima needed to perform a scan to prove that the small blood clots were out of her body, which they were. That was a relief for us. Dr. Ima said, "I will try to wake her up slowly to see how she reacts after this impact."

Oriliz was in an induced coma for three days. Later, the doctor woke her up very slowly and put her into dialysis right away to clean her blood. It took her more than two hours to wake up. Oriliz, in her recuperation, had fourteen dialysis treatments in total, and after that she was out of danger. At that moment, I realized the importance of giving blood, since we can save a life just by donating blood.

After Oriliz got out of intensive care, she spent five more days in the hospital getting her body in top shape with some vitamins and protein her body had lost during the decrease of platelets. Slowly, she was recuperating and feeling stronger each day, until the doctor told us that she could go home. On the way home, she wanted to stop by her grandparents just to say hello and to reconnect with them since she thought that she would not survive. I thought she was doing too much after two weeks in the hospital. She recuperated very fast.

This moment was terrifying for us, and again we lived a close encounter with death. Her case gave me the courage to continue loving my children and caring for them more. I tried to be concerned about Oriliz's health more and more because there was something that bothered me. Again, my intuition was talking to me!

I became closer to Oriliz in everything. I made myself available for her whenever she needed me. Even though she would not listen to me, at least I could give her a helping hand. We had long conversations remembering old times and this time made us closer as friends. Sometimes she would tell me stories, and I was there just listening. I let her be herself. She told me about her coma and with whom she spent the time waiting: my mom. I asked her, "What did she tell you?"

Oriliz said, "Nothing, just that I was not allowed to go with her into the light because it was not my time." According to Oriliz, my mom repeated that many times. Oriliz could not remember the whole conversation, but she remembered the part about the light because she said the light felt so welcoming and pure. She also mentioned that it was a not a bright light that would burn your eyes; it was just an inviting one.

After the danger passed, I thanked God for giving me back Oriliz for the next few years. I felt that I would keep her for a few years and enjoy the beautiful moments with her. Which I did! I did not lose any!

We never missed any appointments after her setback. I asked her if I could go with her to see the results. She nodded, yes. That day was one of the worst days of my life. The doctor told us that her scan showed many small masses in her liver. The masses were caused by the trauma her body had suffered during her coma. Dr. Ima wanted to do more tests to see if it was cancer. Oriliz got upset at God at that moment, saying, "You do not want me here, alive, eh?" and after she approached the doctor, she said, "What should I do? Am I going to die?"

The doctor explained to Oriliz that she would have to do many tests to see the sizes of the masses and that later she would know what to do next.

The return home was silent. There were no words from her or me. We travelled with our mouths closed and probably with turbulent thoughts that we did not know how to control. Later, close to home, I tried to encourage her with words of wisdom, and I think I convinced her. I told her in Spanish, "I am here for you. Just let me know when you will need me, and I will find the way. I am your mom."

Dr. Ima referred us to another doctor, Dr. Leroux. He was an experienced and famous doctor in Montreal. He was a prestigious surgeon recognized by the medical faculty of Montreal University. He was a hematologist and head of research for liver diseases. *La crème de la crème!*

I went with Oriliz to her first appointment to find out about the possibility of an operation. I saw Dr. Leroux for the first time. He was a handsome man with young characteristics, even though he was in his late forties. His hair was black, and he had a skinny body. I came with Oriliz just to listen to what he had to say.

He explained the operation procedure, describing the dangers involved and his skepticism that the operation could be done successfully. I felt he was trying to convince Oriliz to wait and do more tests.

Dr. Leroux fought for Oriliz a lot. He presented her case to the committee as many times as he could, asking for permission to do the dangerous operation. The committee refused him many times. He told me once, "If she had cancer, the operation would immediately be done, but because she doesn't, she needs to wait. I am so sorry, but it is not my fault. I have bosses too." These were his last words to me after Oriliz's death. He felt her death, and he did not want to see me after, but he needed to say that to me. He was dealing with his own nephew's death too at the same time. He lost two people in the same month. I felt his pain, probably not for Oriliz, but I am sure there was something in his soul for her too.

After many visits, tests, and appointments for blood tests, the operation still did not happen. I think Dr. Leroux doubted the operation would be done accurately. He was not sure if everything would be all right. I am sure he was afraid. Or maybe he was afraid of losing his reputation?

Four years passed, with more tests and and more visits to the doctor. The operation was postponed many times without any positive result. I was panicking and getting stressed because my intuition was sending me signs of losing my daughter. Oriliz started getting pain on the right side of her body, close to her liver. The pain was caused by one of the tumours. The tumour grew seven centimetres, and it was crushing one of her ribs, making it hard for her to breathe. Her liver enzymes were increasing in high quantities and the doctor got very scared, telling her that the operation would be the week after her appointment with him. Dr. Leroux prescribed her morphine to calm the pain and gave Oriliz a document for a leave of absence from her work because she needed to be rested before the operation. Before the Friday of that week of February 7, we received a call cancelling the operation again.

"Another cancellation," I said. I was worried because her liver was not waiting. I prayed more and stronger than ever, but Oriliz was feeling sicker. She just wanted to rest and nothing else.

The doctor called us for one last appointment. He explained to Oriliz that she was pregnant and because of the pregnancy the tumour had grown, and was pressing on her ribs. Oriliz needed to do something about that, but the doctor mentioned that would be very risky if he operated. It took Oriliz four days to decide what to do. Believe me; it was one of the hardest decisions that she would have to make—whether or not to have an abortion.

Oriliz felt cheated, disappointed, and saddened by the circumstances. She could not believe what was happening to her. She said, "Mom, I am doing something wrong, no?

I said, "No, Oriliz, you are not doing something wrong. If you are in good health after the operation you can have as many children as you want. This case is different. Your life is the priority; with the baby, it would complicate the operation. Do not worry right now about that. Focus on getting better and stronger."

My daughter was worried she would not kill a human being, her son or daughter, whom she called no name since he/she would not exist. I felt sad for my daughter. I cried and I cried for the fetus because she had always wanted to have a child, and now that she had one, she was in this situation. Oriliz adored children. She always felt good and felt compassionate around them.

Everything was a nightmare that I could not wake up from. And if Oriliz did not survive the operation, what would happen? I would lose my daughter and my grandchild? I was already losing my grandchild... and then... sadness invaded my heart.

Finally, the day of the operation came, and the rest is a sad story...

CHAPTER 7

My Grief as a Mom

I slept so much that I woke up thinking I must go to the hospital. I forgot that my daughter had just passed. I thought, *I am getting too old for this; I am not going to resist it.*

I could not believe that I was back to being alone; the first time was when I left my country, the second time was when I divorced and third time how I had lost Oriliz. I sat down on the bed and started to imagine her in the freezer at the morgue. Panic entered my body and I started shaking. I could not think properly. I wanted to see her, but I knew nobody could help me. I was sad, and at the same time, I was afraid. I didn't know what to do. I felt lonely and vulnerable. I cried dry tears...

I shook my head vigorously and redirected my thoughts to the chores I needed to do, like making appointments with the funeral homes, something I had never done alone or before. This time I needed my dad or my mom to help me. I needed somebody to help me with this situation: someone who would make me feel secure, who would offer me strength. I felt like a child starting a new in life.

I asked myself many times: *Why do I not cry? Why I am so unemotional? Why I am this way?* It was like the inside of my soul became grey, with no thoughts, no feelings, no language, no conversation, just my mind at the speed of light.

Suddenly, blank, pitch black! *Is this what happens when someone dear dies? Is this maybe what others feel?* I didn't know what to think anymore.

My thoughts were all over the place... I started thinking about Oriliz and that I needed to see if she had woken up. I was in denial. I could not believe she was dead. It could not be. She and I had gone through a lot of troubles together, a lot of nightmares about money, and other difficult situations that ended up in an operation. I started panicking. Just thinking that she was alone, and I was not there. Anxiety invaded my body. I could not breathe...

I needed to go out, and I left without a destination. I went around her house to look for her, around her workplace to see if she would come out to tell me, "Mom, you're here!" I didn't know what to do. I was desperate. I began stopping in parks to cry my heart out by myself, screaming her name, *"ORILIZ!"* I didn't care if people were in the park. Now what I wanted was a miracle. I waited... no miracle. I did this for many months and still... no miracle

She died on a Friday, so I could not do any chores until Monday. I thought if I hurried to do my chores she would probably show up after that. It was a nightmare. I wanted to see her as soon as possible, but it was impossible... more waiting...

I was always thinking, more now than ever, *This cannot be happening to me. I do so much. I help people. I try to do my best on this earth. I guess it is not enough. What did GOD want to show me with my daughter dead? Why did he punish me this way?* All these thoughts came out every second, every minute, every hour, and they did not let me relax...

I wanted to go back to work because it would make my mind sane, but I didn't want to hear the people saying: *When my mother died! When my uncle died!* I didn't want to hear anybody talk about anything. I didn't want to hear about death!

Our children think they are superheroes. We protect them as much as we can. The last thing we think is that we will lose them. Something in our mind tells us they will not die first; we are supposed to be the first ones to die. If you see in daily life when we speak about death we always say, "I will go first, then your dad," or "Your grandmother will die first." So reality shakes you in a way that you never could have imagined, and all the laws of the universe invert themselves. Children die first too! Children of all ages die, and we see it almost every day.

I continued my search for Oriliz. I stayed for hours parked at her workplace or in front of her apartment to see if she would come out. I came to the realization that what I was doing was not normal. I had a problem.

I went to the funeral appointment, and while I was checking the cost, my mind was wandering. *I want everything to be perfect for her. Why is that? Why at this moment am I not preparing the perfect graduation or the perfect marriage? Why must I prepare the last thing in her life?* <u>Her death.</u> I screamed inside me: *Noooooo, it cannot be! Augh! Stop!*

For me, Oriliz was the most beautiful thing I had ever shared with the world. She was the smartest, funniest, and most intelligent being, and she came to my life with a purpose: to make us happy for only thirty-two years. Life is so fragile, and we abuse it. We do not even care about the consequences, but they are there, just at the reach of our fingers. They do not go away. I think the hardest part of life for a parent is to have to bury their children. We did not want this to ever happen in our life. And we forget, again...

My mind was changing my beliefs concerning death, and something was telling me to see it from another perspective. I needed to find help since I realized that what I was doing was not normal. I could not continue with life being unfair to me. I needed help. With the help of the Human Resources department at my workplace, I looked for a clinic where I could have some sessions with a psychologist to at least to get out of the anxiety I was carrying around with me. I wanted to stop my mind. I wanted to know why I was not crying, and why I felt this way. I already knew, but I needed confirmation that I was not going crazy. I felt too much pressure from my body: feelings, body aches, and my thoughts. I could not handle it anymore...

Finally, I signed the contract for my daughter's funeral. I was in charge, and I felt guilty. I needed to prepare all these documents which are required by law to make everything proper and documented. I felt guilty again! *What's wrong with me? Ohhhhhh!*

I started the sessions at the clinic. I needed to do ten, and I felt good about it. I began to understand that grieving is a complicated thing. Not everyone grieves the same way. It comes in different forms: as anger, depression, sadness, guilt, etc. According to the person I saw, I might have been experiencing absent, delayed or chronic grief. All of these forms of grief involved disbelief, with no signs of grieving or delayed signs after a long period of time. Whatever the sign if for you, the reality is that one of your children has passed and that is hard to deal with.

I was angry at God, not for what he did to me, for what he did to my daughter. Even though I asked him to change places with me for my daughter's sake, God did not listen. I explained to him that Oriliz was starting her full life, fulfilling her dreams, and reaching her goals with such pride, and then boom.... He ignored me!!

Those were the first days without my daughter. I was going around like a chicken with no head. I could not concentrate, not even on one simple thought. I wanted to discuss with Oriliz what I was doing. That was impossible now. I had this big responsibility, and one part of that was that I needed to remove all her belongings from her apartment. She had so many things; I did not know where to start. I do not think the family even knew how hard it was for me to deal with all her personal stuff without asking Oriliz where it should all go. In the end, with the help of her friends, I succeeded in moving her belongings from her apartment to a storage space I rented. I could store her things there while I started transitioning everything, filling out the documents, making the visits to the government offices and the funeral home—all of this without anybody bothering me. Those moments were my lonely moments.

My thoughts continued: *What about me? I did not want to do anything related to her death. I did not want to do this. But who is going to do it? Who was there capable of handling such a big responsibility? Nobody!* I was the one with delayed grief, according to the woman in charge of my file at the clinic. I needed to do this before the painful trance faded away. Meanwhile, I was fighting to keep myself in control even though my brain was going sideways.

I used to listen to the stories people would tell me about families fighting for properties or money and I never understood it. My brain could not understand how that was possible in those difficult moments. Well, it is true. It happened to my dad, and the man is not even dead. If people can do this with a person who is alive, imagine with a deceased person. I think they take advantage of the situation and the vulnerability of the soul.

You are in your pain, your head is not there, your soul is empty and what goes through your mind is the last moment of your child in the hospital: the warm body becoming cold and the face with signs of the final attempt at revival done a few minutes before. I thought, *What part of grieving do those people who want money and belongings not understand? Is this the right moment to discuss how much money she left and what should I take from her belongings? NO!* My head was going in circles trying to find some logic in my daughter's death. I guess in other people's minds curiosity kicked in, but my mind was not there to think logically.

Whatever she had, it was because she had attained it with effort. She worked for it; she earned what she had. I could say that I contributed to some of her belongings, maybe her dad too, but I needed to decide what I would give away and what I would keep since she had wanted to give everything away; but that was one of my least worries at that moment.

Anyone in their right mind would realize I had a huge pain in my heart and that the last thing I wanted to worry about was her things. I had so much respect for my daughter that I could not abandon everything just to look through her personal belongings; this made me sad. The last thing I wanted to do was start getting weaker by being flooded with memories. *Not now!* I thought. *I will worry later.*

Again, I had so much respect for my daughter. I admired her so much for all that she had accomplished at only thirty-two years old. She was always on top of a pedestal to me, especially since 2010, after her first close call. She knew how helpful and important she was to me. I told her that many times, and I never got tired of telling her. She was everything to me. Maybe it was because I didn't have any family living with me that my two children became my closest friends and companions.

I think I was a role model for my children. I wanted to continue being that role model even though she was dead. She knew I could handle this. I started organizing myself and started preparing everything related to the funeral. I even created a spreadsheet for every expense. At the same time, I was covering myself from accusation from anybody who might dare to invent that I had behaved in an untrustworthy way.

I am a very honest person, and I would never do that to Oriliz. I was very skeptical about death and everything that comes with it, but there is no denial, there was a force helping me from the other side. This is what I believe happened. Let me tell you:

First, the funeral home where we went did not have a room for the day we wanted. When I went to choose the day, the lady offered another day because that particular funeral home was full, and she wanted us to take the one in Villeray. My mouth fell open in disbelief because I knew how Oriliz loved Villeray. She was living there, and she always wanted a house in Villeray. That was my first sign that she was around.

Second, we chose a big room for at least fifty people, thinking that Oriliz as a young person did not know too many people. When we got to the funeral home at Villeray, they had reserved us a room for twenty-five. We kept the room because we were stuck for time. The hall was crowded. It was full and it was right. Everyone was there who had been touched by my daughter's heart: her family, the nursing community, her friends, her school and high school colleagues, her work colleagues, her bosses, her superiors, her teachers, her principals, representatives of the nursing association and the union, and many more who felt at least a little close to her.

Third, the Facebook page and funeral home website were full of messages, from everyone living outside of Canada, the ones who could not attend, and even the ones who did. In my eyes, I could not believe it. This had a huge impact on me. Even though I knew my daughter, I did not know she had such a big impact on all those people. She had touched each one of their hearts in some way. She was very charismatic. She was loved.

Fourth, we had been offered a catholic priest to perform the funeral mass, but the priest cancelled and someone from the funeral home performed the service. The service was perfect; the way she would have liked it. Since Oriliz was not very religious—she was more of a philosophic type—the speech was perfect. The preacher spoke more about life and death. He took some quotes from the book *Blink: The Power of Thinking Without Thinking* by Malcolm Gladwell. It was about how life is very sensible, and we should enjoy it more now rather than worry about the future. It was more about choices in life that are made in a blink of an eye. It was the kind of speech that Oriliz would have liked. The whole thing was perfect: the best for her soul!

All the things that were planned were planned by her; I am sure of that. She wanted everything perfect—her way of perfect—and it happened! I even buried her in her favourite dress: a blue silk dress with white roses that she had purchased a few months before for her trip to Scotland. She looked beautiful!

The room was full of pictures and flowers. "Burning," a hauntingly beautiful piano composition by Ludovico Einaudi played at the same time as the screen of the TV with her life story. Oriliz had chosen that music three weeks earlier in the living room of my apartment. The music, the scent of the flowers and the sadness of the faces imprinted my soul. How could I forget?

After the funeral, Oriliz's body was sent to be cremated. We waited a month to have Oriliz's ashes. While I was waiting for her ashes, I thought about her every day of my life. Every little item of mail reminded me of her. Every phone call I made on her behalf reminded me of her. Not one day went by without thinking or talking about her. On the days that I was not thinking, she made sure I remembered her because something would come up: a song on the radio, a smell of flowers in the car, or strange things without explanation. I knew that she was always there with us.

After the preacher's speech at the hall, I became more aware of life after death. The anxiety and the panic attacks I had been experiencing started to slow down after two friends from work, Josiane and Lorraine, provided me with some spiritual books to read when I had some time. One book was by Sylvia Browne, called *Life on the Other Side,* and the other was *Spirit Messenger* by Gordon Smith. The world I knew was scary, where ghosts follow you just to give you goosebumps and make you feel uneasy. These two books opened my mind to another world that I knew but had kept hidden.

I devoured those books in a day or two. I became obsessed with the afterlife. I read other books: *Proof of Heaven* by Eben Alexander, M.D., *Conversations with God* by Neale Donald Walsch, *Life After Life* by Raymond Moody, and more. When I found the time, I watched online videos and talks about the afterlife. I could not get the subject out of my mind. I saw, on YouTube, the videos of Dr. Elizabeth Kubler–Ross and Dolores Cannon and I discussed them many times with my co-worker Lorraine.

Mrs. Cannon explained a variety of stories about death and souls. Every one of those books and videos that I read pointed me to my daughter's death. I think as a parent, I wanted to hear that my daughter was not afraid and that she was not alone. I guess those books and videos confirmed that.

I started to become more spiritual. I wanted to know more about life after death. I became obsessed with books related to this subject. Oriliz's death had been the worst day of my life. I wanted to see if there was life after death. I wanted to know where my daughter was, and if she was okay. *Is she with the other members of the family, like some books and interviews mentioned?* I wondered. I was changing my mind about everything concerning death. I needed to look for answers. I just needed to know more about this other world, and that is when my spiritual journey began.

CHAPTER 8

Death

On September 27, 2011, my daughter wrote a working paper, in French, about death, as part of a nursing course about caring for the dying, for the Community Health Certificate at the Faculty of Continuing Education. The working paper was named, *"Individual reflection of my family."* I have translated it here to English to show you how my daughter thought about death a year after she had a near-death experience, and four years before her own death. It starts like this:

> Death: a difficult enough subject to tackle. Compared to my Venezuelan and Italian origins, I deeply believe that Quebec culture perceives death differently. From the time I was little, death has been a taboo subject in my family. The less we talked about it, the less likely it would happen...
>
> My mother lived in Venezuela for a few months during my childhood. She later decided to come back to Quebec.
>
> My maternal grandmother died a few months after my mother's arrival in Quebec. She often tells me that she left Venezuela because she had quibbled with her mother. The relationship they had was not the best. My grandmother told her that the day she will die, she will

never be able to come and join her on her deathbed. Indeed! My mother was never able to go there when she was sick. My mother will never forgive herself.

Last week, for the first time, I asked her how she felt about Grandma's death. This time without crying, my mother answered me that she regretted not being able to apologize to her mother for their quibble. Even though I had only seen my grandmother once when I was five, I cried for five days. It had been eleven years since I had seen her. Why cry so much? I think it was the pain of not being able to talk about it and not being able to tell her that I loved her.

All my life, I wanted to be cremated because I found the makeup of the dead bodies in the coffin to be horrible.

When I went to Venezuela to see my family, around the age of twenty-two, I saw a Venezuelan funeral, and right away, I thought about my grandmother. The men carry the body from the church to the cemetery on foot, and the rest of the family are behind the coffin crying while others are singing. I wanted to go that way for her!

Instead, at the Italian funeral, we line up to make the sign of the cross in front of the deceased and make a prayer. Then, to continue, we must offer our condolences to the whole family (spouse, children, and grandchildren). Then, we sit for one hour and finally leave. It is extremely boring and long! Ah! I forgot! You must be dressed in black.

I remember my father's ex-spouse, who was from Quebec, dressed in pink to go to a funeral. She was shown the door at the funeral without her having the time to offer her condolences.... She had not respected these people because she was dressed in pink. I found that very insulting!

I found the Venezuelan funerals so beautiful and less cold than those of the Italians.

Last year I had an idiopathic thrombocytopenic purpura. I almost died after I stopped breathing in the emergency room. Intubated for three days, I saw a light, warm and inviting. My grandmother was there. She spoke to me for a long period. I wanted to go join her, but she did not want me, answering me that it was not my time but that she would watch over me.

My boyfriend saw me going to the resuscitation room. I later learned that he waited two hours before someone informed him of the situation. It is appalling to keep people waiting for so long. Then the workers wonder why the family wants to break down the emergency doors when they have no information.

It was after I awoke in intensive care that I decided that at my funeral I would like to be in an open casket. About death, I do not want to talk about it, but I am less afraid of it. I now understand why rituals are important, that they allow you to grieve healthier. That is what I want for my family when I die. I want them to find it easier to see me go, together and united.

After my daughter passed, one of her friends provided me with this paper. I was in shock when I read it, and I found out that she was ready for her death. There is no explanation of why she wrote this paper. But the paper helps me to understand a little about her funeral. Oriliz never left a will and the paper was kind of my answer. I did have an open casket for her, and I did cremate her. Those were the two words that I wanted to hear. I thought right away that Oriliz was there guiding me.

In my early days living in Venezuela, death was a taboo subject; we would even make the sign of the cross when we pronounced the word *muerte*, meaning "death" in Spanish. It was like this for years, and I think it still is. I now consider death as a rebirth instead. When we die, we go back home, and we see our family that left us first. I have been reading and researching this for so long, and I am convinced that it is not as bad as people think it is. The only part conjoined with death is the suffering, the pain, and the hurt that the person who died left to us here in the physical realm. Some people can get over it quickly, but others can even lose their lives because of it.

One of the books I read about life between lives was *Journey of Souls* by Michael Newton, Ph.D. In this book, you read about how death is a resurrection of the soul again and again. Furthermore, you read how the souls live in heaven after their body has died. These are the experiences of people who had gone to see Dr. Michael Newton for a cure for some of their fears or obsessions. By mistake, Dr. Newton found out that the patients had more to tell. So, he started documenting their experiences, and he found out more than he ever imagined. He found out about life after death. The book is very interesting and skeptical at the same time, especially for those people that think we are just here living life and when we die everything finishes. There is nothing wrong believing that! But, sometimes, I wonder if all that Dr. Newton mentions is possible. Then again, why not? There are many things that we do not know about death and it is difficult to find the answers.

Scientists and medical doctors try to find out answers about death, or even how to stop the process of getting older for that matter, but with no results, They just have different opinions and no definitive conclusions.

I think we came here to do something that makes us grow as souls. There are things that we cannot explain that sometimes happen. Now, I believe one hundred percent that there is no coincidence to all the things we do. They need to happen for a reason; maybe the reason is for us to do things right and better. Maybe we did something one time and it came out wrong; now is the chance to make it better. Sometimes I wonder...

I know that my daughter's death and the pain that I have has nothing to do with all that. But it makes me understand more why a person dies and why we need to stay here continuing doing what we came to do. We are supposed to find our purpose. Don't you wonder sometimes?

Inside me, I was in terrible shape. I showed nothing from the outside or inside, although some people used to tell me that my eyes showed sadness. The trips from work to home were sad. I would start to cry as soon as I opened the door of my house. Just the fact that my daughter had not called me that day, which was for me not normal, would make me cry. It was the end of everything. When you have habits and customs, they are so hard to break, but death suddenly shatters them.

I kept busy after my sessions at the clinic with the social worker I mentioned before. I know people in that state feel like doing nothing, but one of the rules to feel better is to not be alone, to do something instead. Keeping busy with things in the house or outside with friends is the best alternative for a grieving person. Nobody will take away your pain, your thoughts and the way you remember your family member. Those feelings are yours.

My fear during the grieving process was that as time passed, I would forget my daughter. I visited her at the cemetery every day. I used to call the visits "my sanctuary" or "my alone time"; where I used to pass my time talking to her and letting her know that I was there. After watching those YouTube videos and reading those books, my visiting days became less and less. I understood her position and mine. I knew that even if I wanted to spend time with her, she was not there. She has work to do, and places to go. As for me, I needed to continue and finish the life that I came to live. I needed to live in the Now.

My way of acting and thinking about death changed for me. I no longer saw death as an ugly thing. I am not happy either; don't get me wrong; It is a very sensitive subject, especially for the family member. What I am happy about is that the person who died is back home. She or he is not suffering anymore or stuck in a body that is not functional. I am glad that my daughter is not back in her sick or damaged body; even if we want them back, we should think if we want them to continue suffering.

Now if somebody tells me about somebody who is dying or has died, I feel a release in my body. Do not get me wrong, my mind goes back to the first moment when I saw my daughter on her deathbed; but I try to change the subject, or I silence myself. Not because I don't want to talk about it, it is just that not everyone is open to death. My opinions on death might offend people with a more traditional mindset.

One thing you learn in the spirituality classes is to keep your body healthy. It is a kind of gratitude toward loving yourself. How? Keep exercising, eating healthy and loving everything in it. Be grateful for what you have: your health, your house, your car, your children, your food, your job, etc. Thank God, or whatever name you have for the divine, for the things you have, and you will have that are coming your way. The one body you have, it is the shell of your soul. When your body is giving you a sign, you should listen. It is the soul talking to you. The soul that you have is telling you or advising you of any odd moment that you find in your path. Listen! Do not ignore it! I am not a doctor, but I speak from experience. Believe me! What happened to my daughter was not predicted but maybe we could have prevented it. However, it is what it is, and we need to accept it anyway.

After five years had passed, I started to accept my daughter's death. I made peace with God after being mad at him. I understood, even if it was harsh to say it, that some things must happen to make us a better person. From darkness comes the light!

Since my daughter's death, most of her friends changed their lives for the better. They said that life is precious and there is no time to spend anymore being childish. Some of them bought their dream home. Some went for the position they always dreamt about, and some decided to save for a better life. After this painful experience, I think it affected a bunch of people, especially those who adored Oriliz. I don't know what happened to some of them, but I am sure that something happened to them on an emotional level. Like a miracle! It looked like a door opened for everyone. It is a chain of events!

We, as family members, friends, boyfriend, will remember Oriliz as a Good Samaritan. She always wanted them to have what they always wanted, and she was always helping. I will never forget her. I don't think a parent will forget the child who one time made their life shine and happy, full of joy and laughter. I will not forget Oriliz; she will always be close to my heart forever!

After making peace with God, my life, and my daughter's death, I tried to see the whole situation as an experience we needed to confront and to learn something from. I do not want to feel sad. Oriliz was not a sad person; she was full of life and zest. So, I wanted to be like her. I don't know how she did it,.

It took me five years to let go. I took courses in spirituality, which saved me. I am still trying to make life better. I am still fixing the feeling of grieving. I say "fixing" because I will fix it, but I will not cure it.

We cannot forget what it is like to be connected to our child; it is our umbilical cord—the golden thread—the love from you to your child that never disappears even if death is present. That is why parents feel the way they feel toward their children. It is normal! We are connected!

I just want to tell parents whose child passed on to do something memorable for the child. Do it for at least a few years. Do not take your life, because there is something for you to do on this earth: something happy to remember. Live in the present, in the Now. Teach your children good beliefs and be their role model. Remember them for the unique characteristics that they have. Know them. Give them, in the Now, what they need to evolve in this life. Life is hard already; do not make it harder than it is. They need us for anything and everything. They can be older, but in the parents' eyes, they are still their babies. In general, enjoy them now that they are alive. Later, it will be sadness and regret that some of us will bear. Others will carry those feelings forever. Let's teach our children that life matters, starting with your body, loving yourself, and loving others the same way you want to be loved. Your life and achievements will open to a new phase, a better one. You will see the results.

Sometimes I ask God, *Why do I know this now? How come I didn't know this when my daughter was alive? That way I could have taught my children what I just learned—that it is so beautiful and peaceful to keep in their hearts.*

Remember, death is with us all the time, but we want to ignore it and we do not want to know. Death lives among us every day, side by side. We should learn how to live with it, learn not to be afraid and to let go. Everything dies, so, the best thing is to enjoy life fully and memorably and to try not to have regrets at the end of our life. We are attached to the material objects and things in our life. This is the reason why we cannot let go. But we are born alone on the earth and we leave alone. We cannot bring anybody or anything. The body is the physical and the mind is the spiritual, our consciousness continues. Where? I don't know, but I know there is something beyond us that we cannot explain. We should be curious, without prejudice.

CHAPTER 9

My Son, Giovanni

I have another child, a son who was born on August 24, 1984. He was thirty years old when Oriliz passed away. I needed to write about him because I imagine as a mother that Oriliz's death triggered something within him. He was living with me when all this happened. Giovanni decided to move to another apartment to make his independent life. "It's time!" he told me. Before Oriliz passed on she spoke to him and told him to promise her that he would move out of my house. Which he did!

During the time of Oriliz's passing, my ex and I could not get along. He wanted different things, and I did too. So, Giovanni was trapped between two parents who tried to communicate during the whole tragedy. His stress level was high, and at the same time, he was mourning his sister, who I imagine he loved so much. Neither my ex nor I realized at that moment that all of us were mourning a family member.

Since Giovanni was a baby Oriliz had taken care of him. She made sure he crossed the street the proper way and that he followed her big-sister orders. She never let him down. I think my son did more mischief to my daughter than my daughter to him. Giovanni is more streetwise than Oriliz, but Oriliz was more studious than Giovanni.

Giovanni is more creative and imaginative. He loves music, arts and anything artistic. Giovanni dedicates his time to music. He plays the guitar, and since Oriliz's death, he is being more creative with his music than ever before. He tells me that he feels Oriliz when he is playing and the inspiration he gets is because of her. I love that! It is good for his soul!!

I think my son is suffering in silence; even though we spoke about Oriliz's death he always mentions that he already made peace with her death. I think the pain is still there, but he is stronger than all of us, and he has found his own way of coping. We have open communication when it comes to spirituality; there are things that he is willing to accept and others he is skeptical about. All this is good. He does not discard the possibility.

Giovanni was the person in charge of the eulogy after the preacher gave his talk. He said to me that when he went to do the eulogy something came over him, as if somebody was telling him the words. He felt Oriliz. He spoke words of wisdom and love. He thanked the people for being there for us, especially for Oriliz. He mentioned that she touched each of us in a special way.

Giovanni never asked for anything. He kept to himself. He barely mentioned anything after the funeral. I guess it was his way of saying: I am mourning my sister!

I know how it feels, and I know that Giovanni feels the same way, especially since the day that Oriliz died was the day he planned to visit her. He never got the chance to say goodbye or to make a joke for her to keep. In a way, he knows that she knows how much he loved her. She knows, for sure!

One thing, we keep honouring is Oriliz's birthday. We celebrate it on December 21, at the same restaurant every year. She loved Indian food. We gather with friends to have a good time, always remembering her. It has not been easy for any of us, but at least we try to overcome our suffering by doing something nice in her memory.

At Oriliz's fourth anniversary, Giovanni found refuge by going to Iqaluit. Iqaluit is a town in the Canadian territory of Nunavut. He found something different to do for his own peace of mind. He saw beautiful landscapes and the nighttime sky lighting up in different colours—the aurora borealis. He said is peaceful and divine. I guess he feels like me; the urge to tell Oriliz how beautiful the town is where he is staying.

How he dealt with the mourning of her sister's death, only he knows. I just speak from what I have experienced. Differences in grieving exist; maybe my son has a method that for him was not bad. Maybe he understood death before I did. Maybe he made peace with his grief before I did. The only thing I can say is that my mind was not there. I could not help him because I needed help too. Everyone in the family was trying the best possible way they knew to cope with the pain inside. The best part of all this is that my son was not a child; he knew where to go and what to do in case of unhappiness. I am glad for that! It would have been difficult if he had been a child who was depending on an adult to survive. How could we provide moral help to this child? It would have been difficult!

After five years, I see that Giovanni is trying to find himself after the many ups and downs life has brought him. He will find his path. Oriliz will help him find what he really wants in life. Sometimes a devastating situation, such as the death of a loved one, makes you wake up and put your sense in life, in the Now.

Later, you go into the past to see what you did for yourself and others. Then you realize it... and change the whole you.

My son Giovanni and my daughter Oriliz

CHAPTER 10

Her Endeavours and Her Charisma

For those who did not know Oriliz, she was very smart, hard-working, passionate, and enthusiastic about everything she did and touched. She had enthsuiasm for life, for her family and for her social life. She put her friends first and she adored "K." She talked so well of him every opportunity she could. She loved him so much. It was love at first sight. She also loved her work; she did it so perfectly from A to Z that nothing was left undone.

In her early years, Oriliz was a nurse at Sainte-Justine hospital. She worked long hours, and she wanted to prove herself. Later she was moved to infectious diseases, then to the operating ward, and much later to the ER. She learned everything she possibly could and used her experience to move to other related locations. She worked at Maisonneuve-Rosemont hospital during her student training, but in her later years, she worked as a school nurse at the Riviere des Prairies CLSC (a local community service centre in Montreal, Quebec) for a few English schools. She was loved and respected by everyone in those schools. Simultaneously, she was a preceptor at McGill University for the Ingram School of Nursing. There, she took care of many students and trainees. She loved those students; she wanted them to do as well as she had in school. She was sincere with them when she was expressing her concerns.

Oriliz was very straight forward with things that she wanted her friends to know, or anyone for that matter. She took everything seriously, exactly the way it was supposed to be. She did not take anything for granted! She was very assertive in relation to nursing. She was a defender of rights.

One of Oriliz's dreams was to get her university degree and to be a defender of all nurses. She was close to reaching one of those dreams: getting her bachelor's degree in nursing. *One more semester and one hard course and I'm done!* she used to say to me. I am sure she would have been celebrating that one!

She fulfilled many of her dreams. She was successful and blessed in her life because she found all the right people at the right time, and even the wrong people made her stronger to continue in her journey. She always presented problems with solutions. She helped everyone she met on her way. She was an ear for her friends who needed help.

She loved fashion and shoes. She loved buying clothes, exclusive clothes, different per se. She wanted to be the first one to have it. She loved her social life with her friends and family. She loved food, especially Italian. Every holiday she celebrated: Sugar Shack in spring, Christmas, Easter, Halloween, April fools, etc. She was funny and enjoyable for everyone who had interactions with her. She was an adorable person to meet, but when nothing was going her way, or when somebody broke the rules, her bad character kicked in. That was Oriliz. The angel of defence and justice!!

She was a lovely daughter, sister, cousin, grandchild, and friend. She made everyone laugh. She had a portfolio of personal jokes that would make us laugh while she was telling us the stories. She used to do her acts the way it happened, with mimicry, even using the same voice as the person in the joke.

Oriliz came into our lives to make us laugh, to give us tears, anger, and love. She lived her life fully, like an old person who had reached the golden years, with only her thirty-two years. She travelled so much; she was close to knowing the world. She travelled to Portugal, Spain, Italy, Azores Island, Scotland, London, Paris, the Alps, Cuba, Dominican Republic, Florida, Virginia, Atlanta, Louisiana, Chicago, Toronto, Quebec, Venezuela, Margarita island, and more. I lost count. And with these trips also came multicultural friends. She had friends everywhere. My God, I could not believe it!

One of her funny things is when she was at the hospital on January 20, 2014, she wrote a small letter to the hospital that she never sent. I found it in her emails, and it made me laugh. I never laughed so much after her death. I think she left it there with that intention. Imagine if she would have sent it to the hospital administration? So funny! I will share it with you:

> *Dear Hospital,*
>
> *I am ready to devote one week of my time to teach you real cooking. We are talking here about staying traditional in selected dishes from different countries. It is important not to confuse minestrone soup with water. The minestrone soup is a voluptuous soup with a particular taste for tasty Italian spices as well as legumes rich in iron. Also, make sure your food is cooked properly. For example, a pear croustade should be baked.*
>
> *It is with great pleasure that I will share my recipes for a better world.*

I found a binder of her recipes; Oriliz loved cooking. She was creative when it came to baking. She loved sweets and any type of pasta. She was a chef in her own way!

I also found so many letters that she used to send to her work. One of these letters was written on Tuesday, June 18, 2013, for a job offer at McGill University, and this is what she wrote:

> *I will start this letter by saying: What a great year! It was my first year as a Clinical Instructor with the Ingram School of Nursing and I loved my experience!*
>
> *I was always there for the students, selecting me for the prize as Preceptorship/Advising form. McGill's Nursing students just boosted up my love for the job.*
>
> *I was a Clinical Instructor for Community Nursing NUR1-431-003 for Fall Semester 2012 and Clinical*

Instructor for Community Nursing NUR1-432-003 for Winter Semester 2012-2013. I oversee 21 students, leading me to discover a new side to the Clinical Nursing, meeting with preceptors and knowing the settings where students do their practice. I met with preceptors twice in a semester to evaluate the clinical setting objectives and when and how to evaluate their students.

I motivated the preceptors' difficult students because of the lack of knowledge and enthusiasm during their path. I assisted them with the mid-term and final evaluation when they needed it. I also corrected paperwork, ex: <u>The Reflective practice paper and the Clinical Progress note</u>. After the evaluations were final and the paper corrected, I entered the grades in my course's list.

I assisted and guided the students in their CBO project when necessary. I evaluated the project presentations together with other teachers and Clinical Instructors, such as Josee, Anna, and Françoise.

I've been a nurse for almost 10 years and never thought that one day I could become a member of the McGill Nursing staff. I started as a preceptor for McGill Nursing students in November 2008.

I remember being a student, loving to discover new facts and being curious about nursing. After being a Pediatric Nurse I realized that my job was in the community. I started seeking for a job as a Community Nurse and luckily enough, in April 2007, I found at the CSSS Point-de-Ile as Homecare Nurse, when I discovered what Nurses can do in the community! I worked for one a half year in Home care and in November 2008, I apply to Nursing School.

As a school nurse, being so close to our younger generation was the best way for me to promote health. I was working in Elementary schools until June 2012, but since September 2012, I've been working in High Schools with teenagers.

When McGill Ingram School of Nursing asked me if I wanted students from the Nursing school I did remember saying: Yes! Because by having Nursing students it just brings up my motivation, to keep learning because every time I'm with them I learned something new. They were happy to discover a new part of nursing they had never seen. Those shiny eyes with curiosity just made me want to have more students!

Finally, it did happen. I became a staff member as a Clinical Instructor of the McGill Ingram School of Nursing in August 2011 and I started to share my part of the story with my students. I also had a chance to teach a course on Home Care, hoping to do it again!

As soon as I finish my bachelor's degree, I would like to enroll in a master's degree to have more knowledge and share it with others as well with my students.

My goal is to continue teaching as a Clinical Instructor to be there for the students and their clinical settings as I have done in the last year.

I do hope to continue to share my dream, experience, and curiosity about nursing to the new students to come. Thank you for considering my candidature.

Oriliz kept every certificate and attestation for courses taken during her career as a nurse. Any possible interesting training she took: diabetes 1, vaccination for H1N1, treatment for body image and weight, arterial hypertension, abuse and neglect, internet security (medical files), exposure to blood and biological fluids, along with many letters of gratitude for all the vocational training cooperation.

One of the letters sent to her by email on July 10, 2013, said:

Congratulations to *Mrs. Oriliz, nurse, General Service, Youth and Family Branch, and Multidisciplinary Services:*
Description of the good move:
Mme Oriliz, Nurse at the School-Youth program CAFE, had received the Ingram School of nursing award for excellence in preceptorship. This prize is awarded to a supervisor who has made an extraordinary contribution to the training of trainees. The opening to Mrs. Oriliz to even question the practices on the conduct of the trainees and her passion for the transmission of

her knowledge have earned her this recognition. Her conception of internship terms as enriching experiences for both the trainee and the internship supervisor was recognized as an over-service with an exemplary approach.

We would like to express our sincerest congratulations!

We are proud that the contribution of a nurse from our organization is recognized by such a prestigious nursing school. We encourage you to promote the positive effects of the traineeship mandates, both for the trainee, the teacher and the organization, to your colleagues. Congratulations on your dedication to the Training of the traineeship!

This good move highlights the quality of the internship framework offered at the CSSS and ensures the rigorous training of future members of our organization.

Good shot highlighted by Program Manager, General Service, Youth and Family Branch

As a parent, I cannot forget or ignore all her success and that her dreams did come true. I feel like a proud mom of a daughter who one time created her life without any regrets.

Just remember to find all the things that your child did: see it, read it, laugh, admire the pieces of literature or drawings done by them, find the beauty in them. I framed some drawings done by Oriliz when she was in elementary school. I hung them on my office wall. It is a way to remember her, a way to have her close to me.

Remember all the things done by your child. You never know what treasure you will find. Be grateful because that legacy is left to you and maybe to others! You never know!!

There is nothing we cannot say about Oriliz. She was very special in her way! We are grateful for so many things left by her in our life. Thank you, Oriliz, and we always love you.

SCOTLAND 2013

CHAPTER 11

Rest in Peace

There was not much to say at the burial. We, the family, and Oriliz's friends waited for her ashes to come to rest at Saint Francis of Assisi Cemetery. I was at the office signing papers for the funeral home to release her ashes. When the personnel came with the ashes, my ex-husband took them and cried his heart out for at least thirty minutes or more. The pain that enveloped that man was unbearable. He could not resist saying a last goodbye to his beautiful Oriliz. There were no more words to say; just the tears were saying everything there. The tears were describing the pain and the torture, and possibly the guilt of not being with her for her last breath.

I felt the same, but I was in denial. In my mind, I thought that she would wake up and show up the next day, laughing again and joking the way she always did. I wanted to cry in the last minutes, but my tears were inside. My thoughts were my tears inside my brain. My anger and my feelings were my tears inside my body. At that moment, I was feeling weak. I did not know what to do.

I was resting my body against the glass behind her tomb. The rest of her friends were just looking at my ex-husband and how he was crying with despair. Oriliz's friends were also crying in silence. I didn't see their body language, but I know the surrounding was cold and fearsome. The woman spoke, and she said, "It is time." My son approached his dad with a touch on his shoulder to let go of the urn and he gave Oriliz a last hug and kisses. Every one of us kissed her urn and let her go to rest inside the niche. We stayed a few minutes after the silence of affection last. Everyone started leaving one by one. I went to my car and cried without ceasing. I was banging the dash of the car out of anger and despair.

That day was one of the saddest days. I guess for everyone else too. I knew this was the last goodbye and farewell to my beautiful daughter who completed us for many years.

Her death is in our memories forever until our death. Then, let us forget the painful moment that one day will become a happy one when we will reunite again...

CHAPTER 12

My Spiritual Path–The Awakening

The passing of my daughter was devastating for me. I had another face, a face of fear. I did not know how to show my feelings, and I was very afraid of what would come out of me. The pain was insufferable, and it was getting out of control. I was going crazy with all the thinking and doubts that were passing through my mind as fast as the speed of light. I had a chest pain that would not go away unless I cried my guts out. Even though that was the only way to alleviate the pain, it was not happening for me. Meanwhile, I was trying to keep my mind busy with work, but the pain remained...

As I mentioned before, two of my co-workers felt my pain. They offered me two books to read: Sylvia Browne's *Life on the Other Side* and Gordon Smith's *Spirit Messenger*. My mind was blown away, and I was open for more. The books started presenting in my life like a magic art. Different styles of books: spirituality, mediumship, souls, NDE, energy, chakras, the universe, etc. I read them all.

From the beginning, I was skeptical because some stories were like a fantasy from a children's book, others had explanations that were so certain and precise that they looked real. I started comparing my whole esoteric life with some of those books. Then, I started to remember situations that happened to me during my early years. My memory went back...

At the age of four or five, I felt a rush of energy for the first time. I was living on a small street, called San Carlos, in Barcelona, Venezuela. My kindergarten school was on the corner across from my street. My mother used to tell me to walk on the other sidewalk since there was a man giving candies to children, and she did not want me to take any from that man. One day I forgot and took the other sidewalk. As I was passing by his front door, I saw him for the first time. He stood there as if he owned the street. He was a tall man, in his forties or fifties, with white hair and dressed in a *liqui liqui* (a traditional suit wore by men in Venezuela). The old man had a straw hat and *espadrilles* (a type of flat shoe), and he looked dirty and strange in his look. I took a glance to see inside his house, almost empty, no furniture; his décor was very old fashioned, dusty and not clean. Everything was in slow motion. I felt the rush of negative energy which made me run to my house. It felt like it took me forever to arrive home, but my mom was waiting for me and she mentioned again about the sidewalk. I felt safe with my mom. Now I was curious, but it was dangerous. I felt it. I have never forgotten that feeling and the man's face. He must be dead by now, but in those days our parents took care of us, hiding the fact that those men were pedophiles living among children. However, the moral of the story is that I was only a child, and I felt his malice, his bad intentions as fire running through my veins. After that moment, I felt alert; I felt like an adult in a child's body, as if something woke up in me.

Growing up, I always felt that I did not fit anywhere. I felt that I was trying so hard to make friends and acquaintances but always got ejected from a group or any gathering with more than three people. Some friends told me that I was weird. Indeed! I had something that I had never known. During those days I experienced feelings of envy and jealousy from friends; feelings that I never understood, and I never agreed with them.

At the age of eleven or twelve, I had my first contact with spirituality. I went to bed because my sister wanted me to go to bed. My sister was the oldest one and sometimes she took care of us. I was always afraid to go to sleep alone; I always needed somebody with me because I was afraid of the new house we were living in at the time. I always felt something, and I used to hear voices. It was an uneasy feeling. So, my sister decided to go with me since she was tired too. I remember that I could not sleep because I was moving from side to side. Finally, I became tired. A few minutes later, I saw a bright light in the corridor in front of the door of my room. For me, it happened after I closed my eyes. I screamed to my sister to turn off the lights, but the bright light continued in my face, so I decided to open my eyes. I saw that my sister was deep into her dreams, and I directed my eyes toward the door where I saw a beautiful gold/white angel talking to me. My first reaction was to cover my face, but I saw that it was still standing with the bright light that was not incandescent. He was talking to me. I could hear what he was telling me, but I did not understand. Then, I heard a high-pitched noise, like my ears were ringing. I guess the communication broke, and I went to put my hands over my ears. The angel disappeared. At that moment, I heard a rooster in the distance, and I jumped out of bed. I went to wake up my sister Mary and I told her about the angel. She told me it was just a dream. I saw what I saw. It was real for me, and it happened before dawn because I heard the crowing of the rooster. I told my mom about the angel and she said, "Angels come to bring us a message." But what was the message? He was talking to me. But what did he say? I could not remember. I wanted to, but even if I tried I could not. I forgot about the event. I never spoke about it again, and I let it be.

I started to see that I always carried with me something esoteric. I could not figure it out. But I said to myself, *One day, one day.* I used to think about somebody or ask about a person and something bad was happening to that specific person. I think everyone has this type of sense. I cannot explain it, but I have the gift. In my homeland, they call anything weird or inexplicable, "the gift." Sometimes I have dreams that generally happen, not the same way but similar, but I knew it before. When you are not aware of your gift and something of this type happens, you are afraid. You do not know why you are this way and then, you turn it off sometimes.

I have always had my intuition talking to me, but I never paid it much attention. One day, I was trying to brag about my weird feelings in a group of my mom's friends and one of the ladies in the group told me that was not a gift, that it was the devil who dresses as an angel or gives you false dreams to make you believe and to get you away from

God. I did not believe her. Come on... But it made me realize that not everyone agrees. So, I have to be careful.

I was never a religious person myself. I used to frequent different churches, but I never felt anything sensational for me to stay. I was always asking God the question, *Where is the church you want me to join?* I never got the answer! I always asked myself this question: *Why he did not answer me?* I think it is because there was never a church for me to belong to because God is freedom! God is everywhere!

I have always had an intuitive personality. I always see more than normal, and I could feel the energy of the people interacting with me. Sometimes, I could not understand the energy I received because the person interacting with me appeared as a nice person but with bad energy. I could see more than just energy. I could feel the emotion a person had toward me: if she hated me or had good intentions. I could feel them all. I started to block myself off, personally and spiritually, because I could not have a healthy relationship if I was feeling the vibrations of the other person. I ignored my intuition for a while. But it was the wrong thing to do...

All around my teenager and adulthood years I had different experiences and encounters with spirits in person and in dreams. I felt death in people around me and sometimes I had premonitions before it happened. I cannot explain specifically why I have this but now I realize that we all carry one or more gifts: claircognizance, clairaudience, clairvoyance, clairsentience, clairolfactance, precognition, psychometry, telepathy, etc. At least, we carry one of them!

After my divorce, I met a French Canadian, a handsome blond man with blue eyes. His name was Andres. I spent five years of my life with Andres until we decided to separate. In the third year of living together, his father passed. I was always by Andres's side before his father died and during the funeral. I remember that we were looking for a pair of shoes to bury the man and we could not find them; so, we buried him without shoes. After the burial, we went to a restaurant and then home. We were so tired that we decided to go to sleep. I remember that I could not sleep, and suddenly, I saw his father floating in front of me and talking to me about his shoes. He had a bible in his hands and a candle with a dim light. I felt regret and sadness at the same time. He was telling me to pray a lot for him and to light a lot of candles for him since he was in the dark, and he said to bring a pair of shoes to his tomb; it would make him happy. I woke up Andres and I told him the message. Andres did not want to believe me but we did what his father told me the next day, and we kept lighting candles and praying almost every day.

At the end of 2014, the year of my daughter's death, I was putting my mind more into the afterlife. I wanted to see my daughter again. I wanted her to speak to me and tell me that she was all right. I was continuing to have more insights into the spiritual world. I felt this was my path. I felt that I was a kind of lightworker. I just did not see it, but one day I knew I would wake up and see it with my own eyes.

For those who want to keep their mind closed to what we are, the universe will give you the opportunity to wake up. Whatever is meant for us, it will come to us. If we are open to receive it...

I mentioned before that I have dreams that, in a way, come true with a different scenario. I live my dreams like I am part of them, and I interpret them the way I feel them. The concepts in my dream, become somewhat true. Sometimes I am accurate in the results, sometimes not so much. But eventually, they happen anyway!

In 1996, I had a dream about one of my godmother's children. In the dream, her oldest son came to visit me in Canada with his father. He told me, *I came to see you to say goodbye.*

I said, *"Come in. How come you didn't say anything that you were here?"* and he started backing up like something was pulling him back, He disappeared into the dark with his father who was at his side. I woke up perspiring, and I reached for the phone to call my father in Venezuela. I realized that it was one or two o'clock in the morning there.

My father told me, "Ah, Liz. Who called you?"

I said to him, "Nobody. I had a dream." And I start telling him about my dream. He told me, crying, that Everett had an accident and his parents went to see what had happened.

I told him, "He is dead. He is dead." So he was.

What happened that night, I cannot explain. I am sure he came to say goodbye. Everett and I were very close friends. I was shy in front of him, and he was a funny guy who made me laugh. His way of talking made me laugh. I had a crush on him!

Another time, in 1997, when my mother was sick, I felt it. I began calling at the beginning of November to see how she was feeling. No answer. I tried many times, the next day, the next week: no answer. I called for her birthday: no answer. I knew that something was wrong, but nobody wanted to tell me. I could not speak to anybody. My body felt it. It is a feeling that something is disconnecting from your body. I do not know how to explain the feeling, but it is if the soul is in pain talking to you. My mother got sick at the beginning of November and she died on the thirtieth of that month. I wanted to speak to her for the last time. No success... I said farewell to my mom from where I was: Canada. I could not see her, and everyone in my family had a story to tell about her death. Everyone's perception is different. Mine is that her death was caused by lupus and we cannot deny that she had many years on cortisone, the miracle pill which slowly kills. I have the disease myself, and I know now how my mom suffered from this disease. In those days there was not much she could do. Cortisone was the best treatment at the time. I felt my mom's death; I felt it a few days before it happened...

Sometimes, I remember a person or just their name, and when I ask, I discover that person has gotten sick or dies later after a sickness. It is so strange that we have the intuition and that specific energy that connects us with others. We think all this is weird, but it is not. We have the power to feel any energy, especially with those we often frequent, the ones we love and even the ones we hate, because we all are connected by energy. We all are!

In 2010, I had a dream that my daughter was full of bruises all over her body and she ended up in the hospital. I felt agony and despair, and my heart was beating fast as if something bad was going to happen. Her boyfriend at the time had a very harsh personality when he wanted to get his point across, so I thought my dream was about him sending my daughter to the hospital because of a disagreement. I was wrong. My dream was about my daughter getting sick with purpura. That was the time she first ended up in the hospital and almost died. My question is: Why did I have that dream? Was God letting me know about my daughter's disease to prevent it? Maybe. Sometimes we get answers, accurate answers, but because we do not put any attention to our dreams, thinking that they are not real, everything falls into nothing.

In 2012, we got an invitation to a wedding in Italy. A niece of my ex-husband was tying the knot. My daughter and I planned to go. My daughter planned the trip and the places to visit, and I was the one paying. She studied about the whole northern part of Italy for places to go during our stay. She planned for us to arrive in Rome and have a car rented to go to Milan where the wedding was being held. She wanted to visit the little villages around the outskirts of Milan. We stopped in Siena, Assisi, Pisa, Viterbo, Bologna, San Gimignano, Livorno, Perugia, Florence, Genoa, Milan and then Venice as a day trip. I loved it! In Florence, we went to find the hotel, which was in a crescent close to a big road near the highway. The man brought us to the room. The weather was humid and wet, and it was a little chilly. I entered the room, and I felt right away a rush of energy and the scent of flowers: my sign of somebody dead. I felt the temperature to be very cold, but my daughter said that it was fine. The whole room was decorated like the 1930s: an old-style wooden bed, an antique dresser, even a chair in the corner. My daughter went downstairs to the lobby right away to connect to the Wi-Fi. I stayed in the room, which was not easy for me since I felt that somebody was looking at me. I dressed fast, and I went to rejoin my daughter. I lied to her, saying that I was hungry and that I wanted to take some pictures of Florence. She finished her conversation online and we headed off to Florence's downtown. The street was crowded. It was full of tourists dressed in a variety of colours with cameras and phones. I loved the Ponte Vecchio bridge which spans the aggressive river, Arno, to connect one part of the city with the other. We did not spend too much time walking around since we needed to leave early the next day. We went back to the room, and we prepared ourselves to sleep. We were exhausted and right away we slept, until... the bed started to move like a cradle. I felt it first, and I opened my eyes to see an old lady, Italian in appearance, wearing a long black dress with a grey cat on the side. She had a mean look, and she was saying in Italian to leave her house. She did not want us there. She continued moving the bed until Oriliz woke up and told me to stop moving the bed. I looked at her and I said in low voice, "It is not me; it is the lady behind me. She is dressed in black and she wants us to leave the room."

My daughter said, "Really?"

I turned around and saw that the lady was still there. The tiredness reached me first, and I fell back asleep.

The next day, we asked at the reception who the woman was in the picture, and he said, "The owner of the house."

I said, "She was in my room yesterday."

He answered me, "Your room is in the original house. This part here is new."

Oriliz and I laughed; she took it as a joke. We had fun. It was one of the best vacations I had with my daughter.

In 2014, I felt the worst feeling of my life. I felt uneasy from the beginning of Oriliz's operation until the end, at her death. I knew something was wrong. I did not see or dream anything beforehand. I was feeling in my blood like something was invading it. It just felt strangely uncomfortable. I felt cold all the way through. My brain was giving me thoughts of true, but it was unreal for me to believe them. My legs were weak but strong at the same time. My body was shooting feelings of negativism and positivism at the same time. My body was acting at one hundred percent in all its elements together. I was exhausted, but at the same time, controlling myself not to faint. I could not understand what was going on, but finally, the truth came out: my daughter died. My soul was talking to me, preparing me for a painful loss.

In 2016, I felt the presence of somebody. My body felt scared. I knew the feeling, but I was not sure since the person was alive. I had a cousin living with us during my teenage years. I feared him. I panicked when he used to see me with those weird eyes. I lost contact with him once I came to Canada. I did not know anything about his life. Sometimes I used to hear a story here and there about him, but that was it. I used to call my sister and she used to tell me that he did not do much, he was always drinking and crazy the way he always was. My sister told me about something that happened to him. She said that he was at a party with my cousin's family and he got drunk. All of a sudden, the husband of the daughter of one of my cousins got angry for something he did, and they started fighting. They fought until he ended up in the hospital and then, as per my other cousin, he disappeared from the hospital. I told my sister, "He is dead. He died.

My sister said, "Probably."

I said, "No, he is dead." And I told her about what I felt and that he had come to me in my dreams.

In the dream, he was telling me, *I am sorry for treating you bad and now I will reward you with the best love possible; somebody who will give you what you deserve: true love.*

I felt weird and sad at the same time, because of the story he told me. Maybe he is not dead, maybe he is around the city somewhere. Who knows! But what I felt was a feeling of closure...

Since Oriliz's passing, I have been having dreams, premonitions, glances of different feelings and signs. I do not see myself the same as I was five years ago. I have learned that coincidences do not exist. Everything happens for a reason, meaning that all the weird experiences, the supernatural experiences I had after my daughter's death, were happening for a reason. She is there communicating with me. She is always there when she wants to be.

In one of the dreams I had after her death (well, I called it a dream but it occurred during that period between sleep and awake), I saw her in a blue dress, with long hair, floating above me. I felt the happiness and peace that she brought with her. She gave me thanks for doing what I did for her. Everything that I did, I did it well and perfect, how she wanted. She told me to say hello to her brother and to help her father because he was still sad. She needed to move on, and his sadness was not allowing her to do that. After I spoke to her I felt sadness in my heart, and I started to cry. I saw her and I felt her. I can say now that she is at peace!

Since 2015, I have been studying about energy and everything related to energy. It is a vast subject and if we are open-minded, we can understand the whole concept of energy. One of the books I read, I cannot remember the title, the author was explaining the feeling when you find a soul mate. She explained that when such a relationship is encountered our soul feels as though fireworks are exploding inside us. She repeated many times that we need to experience such energy to believe about love. Our energy sends messages to our body, and probably to our intuition, for us to know if he/she is the one. I would like to feel that...

I started looking for courses and classes related to the unknown. I found Mindvalley Academy. I took a few courses online: duality, unlimited abundance, Silva Life System and the introduction of love and above. These courses opened my mind to a new and unknown topic. I learned how energy works in the earth with us as humans (in the physical realm) and how energy works in the soul (in the spiritual realm).

All the time we interact with a person, the energy crosses between us and that person; there, we see the signs of pleasant or unpleasant energy. They are some people who can see beyond that energy, and may have an accurate perception of the person. I can say that I have done that!

In the winter of 2017, I had some visitors from my country, Venezuela. We decided one day to visit Beaver Lake in Mount Royal. This is a human-made lake in the middle of a big park that freezes over in the winter and is used as a skating rink. Families gather there to enjoy the winter weather. At that time, the temperature was around negative thirty-two to negative thirty-six degrees Celsius, if I remember clearly. It was so cold that we could not stand outside for long. We decided to take a picture in front of the slate which stands magnificent at the entrance of the park. I screamed, "Let's take a picture of the Hernandez family." We stood there for a photo that somebody took for us. What the picture revealed was surprising. Behind us was a bright white light, as if somebody was rushing in to be part of the picture. In the second picture, the orb moved to the front of the slate. I could not believe it! But when I mentioned the Hernandez family, I am sure it was my daughter announcing her presence to all of us. God blessed the moment!!!

One thing I also learned is to be present in the Now and to let go of the past. This part was hard for me. It took me a lot of exercises to get rid of the memory of my daughter's body, the last time I saw her in the cold room. It was a persistent memory.... Now it is just a blurry picture...

I learned how to communicate with my guides and my intuition, since all of us have a guide for our life path. We forget but when we were children we used to pray to our guide: "Angel of the guardian, sweet company. Do not forsake me, neither night nor day." I translated this to English, but I used to say this prayer every night before going to sleep when I was a child. The guide's job is to make sure we follow and succeed in our life path. They protect us. Some people say that it is your intuition. I am not sure about that!

I learned how to meditate and to do it religiously. I tried to do it early in the morning after my gratitude. I learned that you need to love yourself first and take care of your body since your body is the vessel of your soul. Without a body there is no existence in the physical realm. I do exercises in the morning four days a week after my meditation. I practice some exercises on how to manifest some desires, but I am still working on this. I perceive exactly what my reality in this world is.

We, as humans, perceive different realities. We have seen what the matrix wants us to see. Now, I have changed my perspective on life. I could spend time here explaining what I see. How beautifully I see things now. I take in my surroundings in an open-minded matter. How different it is.... The good thing is that I am glad to see it now before I die...

I understood what a belief is. Beliefs are all the things we learned from whomever has been in our life since we were children: our parents, teachers, priests, friends, siblings, etc. We apply those beliefs in our life, and they are not ours to use. We, as humans, have our brains thinking all kind of things. I didn't know that what we have in our mind, negative or positive, we put up there in the universe and that is what we manifest. That's why our beliefs stop us from fulfilling our dreams. The fears, the whole combination of feelings, including jealousy, envy and lust and the everyday expressions in our conversation, our apologetic attitudes, and the words we use to satisfy our surroundings are words to give us some setback in finding success and fame. It is true that there are people with a lot of success, but the success that I am talking about it is freedom and love...

I also learned about crystals and the power they hold for us as humans on this earth. Each crystal has the power to emanate protection or radiate energy for those who need it. That's why humans sometimes need to return to nature, to connect with the trees, to regenerate our bodies; nature has the secret energy that makes us all dynamic.

All these successful subjects made me find my path. I feel more energetic, I have a sense of direction, and I am decisive about how to confront situations and time. The more I understand about energy, the more I realize how important life is, and how energy contributes to my own life and of those around me. We all are responsible for everyone's role on the earth.

Above all, one of the important factors is <u>gratitude</u>. We are supposed to say thank you for everything that we get on this earth, even the bad moments in life. The gratitude will make energy flow to something better. We do not have to compare ourselves with other people, but we can take their experiences and say thank you. One way or another, their experiences affect your life. Sometimes our experiences, good or bad, bring a change of direction to us. We see what is in front of us, but we do not see what is done behind us or around us by the universe. So be grateful for everything, good or bad, without judgment!!!

Every experience teaches us something if we live it because something in us needs to be awakened. We do not know it unless we see it. We must be attentive to the signs and the synchronicities that the universe is putting up there for us. The message is there; just be open to it. About those synchronicities, when you experience them you will be amazed by how great and vast the universe is. There is something up there talking to you. The universe speaks with numbers, quotes written on walls, or any sign in the street. You just need to believe. Trust and you will see! One way to put your doubt to work, if to ask a question to the universe, your guide or your angel and just wait. You could see miracles but be attentive to your surroundings. You may get the answer!

One of the many books I read was *Zero Limits* by Joe Vitale. In it, he explains the process of *ho'oponopono*, the Hawaiian practice of reconciliation and forgiveness (*ho'o* means "to make" and *pono* means "right." The repetition of the word *pono* means "doubly right" or "being right with both self and others." I learned a lot from this book. The whole process of *ho'oponopono* is to take responsibility for every action of everyone on Earth. We all are responsible for everything that is happening. If a message came to you, you did something for that message to be on your computer; that is what Joe explained in his book. If one member of your family is sick, you collaborate with something which makes that person sick. We, as humans, need to take responsibility for everything happening around us, even around the globe. These four phrases: I love you, I am sorry, Please forgive me and Thank you are the key phrases in *ho'oponopono*. The book helps me with my resentment toward my daughter's death. I was angry and I blamed the doctors, the hospital and even God. Now I understand that I must take some responsibility for her death too. Since then, I started to ask for forgiveness, not only for my daughter's death but for other things in life as well. Believe me, it helps...

What I have learned from all these books, articles, magazines and videos is the one frequency: the frequency of love. All of them say that we need to vibrate with the feelings of love. When love owns our lives, love spreads to our surroundings as well. Love changes people's state of being. Spread love and you will see the difference...

You may wonder what all this has to do with my daughter's death. I think if all this information was presented to me, it was for me to be a better person. I believe that she guided me to do this. I needed to find something extreme to get out of the pain and the suffering. I found this and I found my daughter. In a way, she is there. I call her and I feel her presence. I know because of the fragrance of flowers in the air at that moment. My mom's fragrance is sweet like candies. That is how I know my mom is with me. That is why I feel good, doing this. I know that I can feel them. It is the kind of contact that is enough for me. The signs are there. We just need to see them and believe them...

I know all this information may sound odd to many people. Many people will be judgmental, and others may think I have lost my mind. I want to tell you my mind is clearer than ever. I know we have intuition, and we do not use it, but just doing it once, you will be amazed by the results.

I think that the people who left us in this world are still here. They left the physical world; they left their sick vessels, but they are in the spiritual realm where it is much clearer than here. Love is the prominent energy in their lives and the more we reach that energy, the more we reach them, in a way. Love—remember that!

Clairvoyants can see them, talk to them and even see how they are living in that realm. They can tell us more specifically about it. We, humans, do not want to believe because we are occupied with everyday life and what is real for us: money, fashion, possession, and chores. We want something more tangible. We believe what we see. We need to be open-minded and accept all that is tangible and intangible too.

I know that life does not prepare you for everything because we are here to learn. Depending on how we are in this life, all the struggles and setbacks are there for us to become stronger, not weaker. After something of this magnitude happens to you like the death of a child, the problems, the bullies, the secrets, the gossiping, the sarcasm, etc. are minimal disappointments that will not affect us since our body is already patched up. It will not break the spirit anymore; it can upset you, but life has a new meaning tomorrow. Now, you occupy yourself with the big picture, death. There is nothing else that will break you. We can handle pains and sorrows. We came here to learn and to experience. We did not come here to gather all the wealth, to use it only for us and to not share it with the world. We are supposed to share money, food, clothes, even your house, at least one time if the situation comes to your doors. Do not be selfish, be grateful. Give and the universe will multiply for you. Give and do not look to whom you give. Give with love without judging the person, and you will see.

I am happy now. I found my peace. I found myself love. I feel good physically and mentally. I made peace with my daughter's death while I was writing this book, and I understand also about the spiritual realm. Sometimes I have a sad feeling here and there, but it passes easily: not like five years ago when panic attacks invaded my body for a long period of time. I just think about good moments, her face, her smile, and everything comes back to normal.

One of signs to me was the song: "All of You" by John Legend and sometimes "Hello" by Adele. Lately, I have found the iPad opened and playing the song "Fantasy" by Earth, Wind & Fire since she loved that song. I recognize her signs and I check them right away. Somebody else may not believe it, but I get amazed every time!

I know that when somebody dies we stay here on Earth suffering for that person. We miss the person so much, every gesture and every habit. But the truth of the matter is that they are happy. They went back home. They are happy that they are not suffering anymore. You know, we are all going to die. That's the truth! Accept death as a normal step in your life. Talk about it with your kids. Make it a normal subject of conversation, not taboo. That is why death is dark and tenebrous because nobody talks about it, but death is enlightenment.

You do what feels good for you. Do not let people dictate your life. Feel free because we are free beings. We are lightworkers who came to Earth to learn and to grow physically and spiritually. We came to have our children and to guide them into their lives. Our children do not belong to us. They belong to themselves. They should be independent and have a good attitude toward life. My daughter was! And I am happy about that. Now I see it, and it makes me feel good as a person and as a spiritual being.

I know that I will miss Oriliz for all eternity. I feel lonely sometimes, but I know that I am not alone. I have them with me, even though I do not see them. I speak to Oriliz every day. I tell her story and I let her know that I still love her. I get my answers; I see the signs!

Nobody will understand this feeling unless you have a son or daughter close to you who has passed. No pain compares to this. You feel empty, especially when you close your eyes to see their faces again that are not real, that are not there. Children are the most beautiful souls that we can share in this life. They bring joy into your life since they are babies until they are old: from beginning to end.

LIFE IS LENT TO YOU AND IT IS ONLY ONE FOR NOW, SO LET'S ENJOY IT WITH OUR CHILDREN. BE HAPPY, HARMONIOUS AND CAPTURE THE MOST PRECIOUS MOMENTS. BUT ONE PIECE OF ADVICE: LET THEM KNOW THAT YOU LOVE THEM EVERY DAY AND EVERY MOMENT BECAUSE LOVE IS WHAT THEY WILL REMEMBER UP THERE. THE FREQUENCY IS LOVE...

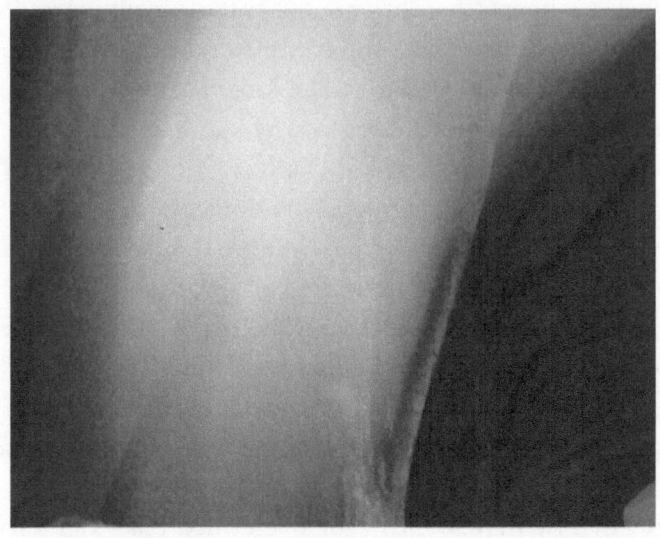

When we took the photo on top of the slate at the park, you can clearly see the shape of an angel or something inside.

In the second photo, the orb was in front of the slate.

For you Oriliz

I dedicate this poem to you
because you are not here,
with the hope you can hear,
to give you the last adieu.

You were missed everywhere,
friends, family, boyfriend.
All of them are at a dead-end
and they think it's not fair.

So many hearts
are feeling the sadness.
They do not want to be part
of this meaningless madness.

From the first day, I miss you
Impossible to forget you,
I guess the time was short
Now and then,
Beautiful days comes to my mind,
Tears and hopes asking when
I will see you again.

I miss that smile,
I miss those jokes,
I laugh for a while,
I scream until I choke.

I ask, I wonder,
Why this all happened.
My head is a thunder,
My heart is wrapped.

The pain created
Doesn't have a name.
While my heart fainted
My body is an ache.

I don't know what to do.
Help me, Oriliz.
Get me out of this blue;
Give me some tips.

While all of us miss you,
Some of us kiss you,
But one of us blesses you
Your dad resists you.

I would like to live there,
Where time is not an issue.
Like that, I will miss you,
Every day, in despair.

Well, Oriliz, all this is
only to tell you,
How wonderful
your life was with us,
How close we were
How I miss your hugs.

Continuing this life,
Not, a clue of tomorrow.
One day at a time
Without any sorrows.

I will see you again with ease,
When I give my back to this world
Screaming your name, Oriliz,
You are my daughter of forevermore.

Love you forever,
Love you more,
Forget you never
Repeat, "encore."

Created by Liz Hernandez (Mom)

I miss you

Every second I miss you,
I think you know that.
There is not a day pass
That I don't see through the glass.

Where my thoughts are going,
Where my screams are faded
I want you to hear them,
for you to trade them.

I cannot do this anymore,
I call for your help
Even though you tore
Even though, you bailed.

The feeling of anguish
doesn't leave my body
The day you vanished
I became cowardly.

The way I feel,
I don't like it at all
Can you make it softer?
Please don't make me crawl.

I wish I could see the future,
I wish I could see it all
To see your beautiful smile,
With no interfering of walls.

In my anguish, I yell,
I guess with this pain
I MISS YOU! Forever
I send you farewell.

Created by Liz Hernandez (Mom)

AFTERWORD

I should be crying in bed for the loss of my daughter, feeling depressed and not having the pleasure of enjoying life as some acquaintances said to me. I should be losing maybe ten years of my life mourning my daughter. But instead, I decided to love life, to embrace what life brings me. There is no point of continuing with this pain if it is only making me sick. I acknowledge that!

The idea to create this book came to me in my dreams. It was a four-year project that I promised myself I would do to find some closure to my grief. In the beginning, I felt embarrassed and ashamed for doing it, since people were telling me that I don't speak proper English. Then, I realized others sometimes struggle to explain a simple situation in English, and I said to myself *I can do this*. I started writing this for those who were judgemental, but I finished it with a feeling of gratitude and appreciation for me, for my son, and for the ones who supported me and my family since we all are creative artists.

In this book, I explained my situation as a stronger person than I am and not as the weak and fragile that I should be. The feelings are real and genuine.

I evoked the feelings as to how Liz Hernandez is. I created this book, as I wanted everyone to see what I went through mentally and to remind people that someone is struggling with oneself for any personal reason.

I am a Venezuelan, proud of my roots, but with a loving heart for Canada too. I always said that I am more Canadian than Venezuelan since I lived in Venezuela for eighteen years and in Canada for forty years.

All the things that happened to me, I never thought would happen. I always judged everything related to spirituality. I judged those speaking aloud about awakening, enlightenment or illumination, but just out of the fear of the unknown. Now, I know that I believe in God more than ever. I think prayers are heard, and they are the ultimate answer to something big. I believe that God is everywhere, but it is up to us to find his love and guidance. I did not know the difference between spirituality and religion. Now I know! Now I can be myself. I can enjoy life and be free.

Awakening by Grief is a book that shows I lived a true path and I am still living it today. I believe all that happened to me and is still happening is the energy of love that is shining on me; it is there, and I see it now. It is protecting us in one way or another. The universe needs your attention and for you to read the signs and to create changes in your life to become illuminated. Once you see the signs and guide yourself to them, you will be awakened. The death of my daughter did not just happen; it was predicted. I believe it was written in her destiny as well as mine.

Why did I choose to come to Canada in the first place? Because it was my destiny—or none of this would have happened.

From 2010, I was aware that she could die, but I did not want to believe it. How could I have prevented it? I don't think I could have prevented it, but even if I could have, the solutions were few. I tried, without success...

There was a bigger message than that: to enjoy life with her all those final years, which I did, and to respect her, love her and enjoy her as my precious child, which I did, to be strong after her death since she will live in me forever, which I did.

I cried with my daughter, I laughed with her, I enjoyed the best and worst moments, and I shared all my life with her. I miss her. There is nothing that I did not do with Oriliz. Today is the day that I get the chance to give her something beautiful and full of love: *Awakening by Grief*.

ABOUT THE AUTHOR

Liz Hernandez is a woman of integrity and honesty whose passion is to be a writer and to help the world with her thoughts and insights as much as she can.

Her talents and achievements increased after achieving her college diploma in language and literature, as they made her more disciplined and confident in her writing.

Liz gained experience as a professional in municipal administration. The active politics in her workplace made her understand that continuous learning is necessary for progress in life.

Liz continues engaging and mastering different disciplines professionally and spiritually for her personal growth and well-being.

In *Awakening by Grief*, Liz describes the discomfort and suffering caused by her daughter's death. Her spiritual belief expanded as she wrote this first book, realizing that her belief was always present and concluding that the universe is the supreme energy, working in our favour.

Her loss and the intangible events of that loss had a big impact on Liz, shifting, transforming and awakening her life forever.

www.ingramcontent.com/pod-product-compliance
Lightning Source LLC
LaVergne TN
LVHW091603060526
838200LV00036B/981